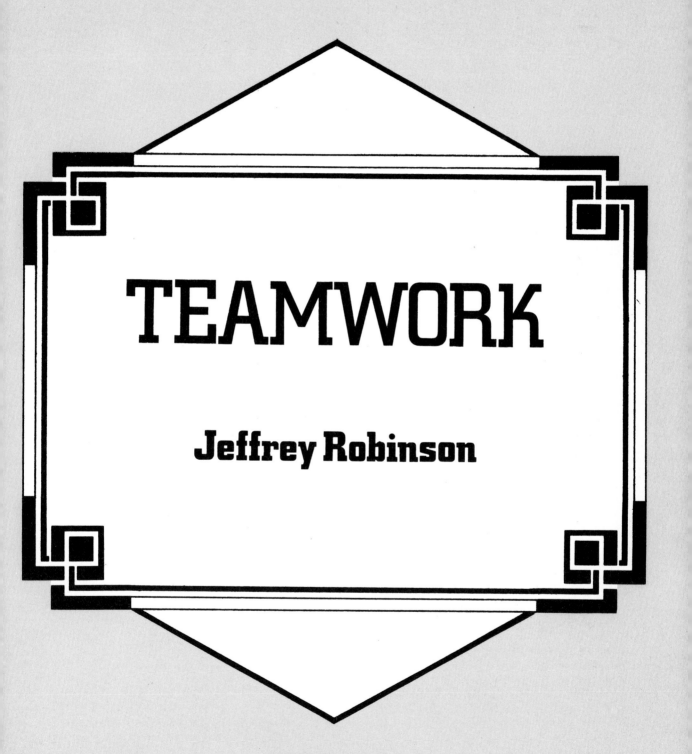

TEAMWORK

Jeffrey Robinson

Proteus

London/New York

All photos courtesy of the Kobal Collection with the exception of the following: pages 9, 21, 43, 48, 55, 80 and 111 – courtesy of the National Film Archieve Stills Library; pages 66-68 – courtesy of the Gate Cinema Shop, Brunswick Square, London WC1.

PROTEUS BOOKS is an imprint of
The Proteus publishing Group

United States
PROTEUS PUBLISHING CO., INC.
733 Third Avenue
New York, NY 10017
distributed by:
THE SCRIBNER BOOK COMPANIES, INC.
597 Fifth Avenue
New York, NY 10017

United Kingdom
PROTEUS (PUBLISHING) LIMITED
Bremar House,
Sale Place
London W2 1PT

ISBN 0 86276 107 7 (paperback)
ISBN 0 86276 108 5 (hardback)

First published in U.S. 1982
First published in U.K. 1982

Design: Adrian Hodgkins
Editor: Kay Rowley
Typeset: SX Composing, Rayleigh, Essex
Printed and bound in Spain by Printer Industria Grafica sa.
D.L.B. 29282 – 1982

Contents

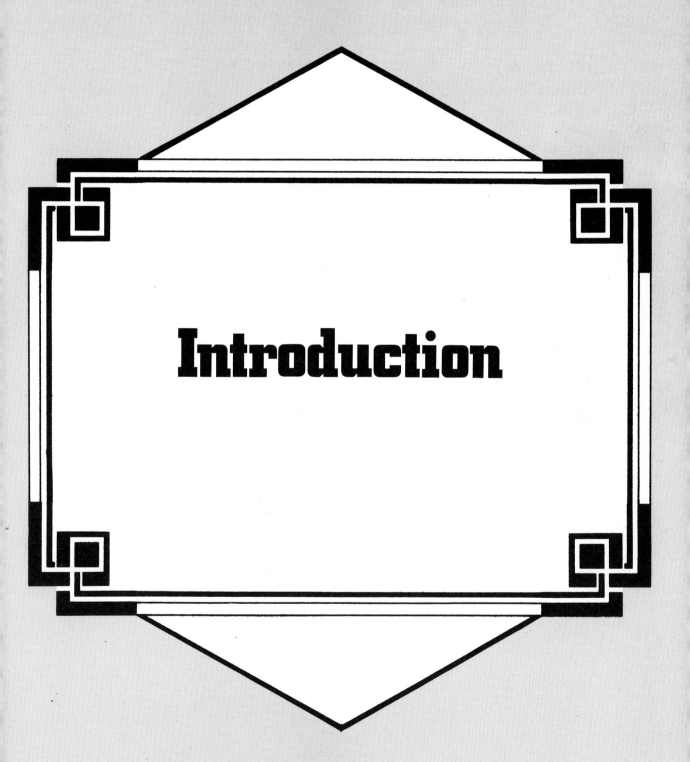

Introduction

We fancied ourselves a team. The world's greatest comedy team. This was long ago. Back in the '50s when teams were in. Back when nine year olds had to be in school every day. And even if we had ourselves convinced that we were the funniest comedy team ever, Hollywood was as far away as the moon. We had to be content with stardom at East School. The closest thing we had to a hit movie was six minutes live at Assembly on alternate Friday afternoons. We thought we were pretty funny as we went through our best routines, all of which were freshly stolen from whichever of those bigger-name teams happened to have been on television the week before. It didn't matter from whom we lifted gags. What counted was that we thought we were as funny as they were. Unfortunately for our career, spelling lessons and math tests and geography books got in the way. Then came the '60s and the world's greatest comedy team . . . at least in East School . . . broke up. We didn't even make the papers . . . although one of us eventually did when he got killed in Vietnam, and another one of us did a few years after that when he became some sort of famous brain surgeon. The other one of us is still plugging away. Hollywood is as distant as it was 30 years ago, although writing a book like this makes it seem just a little closer. Too bad we had to grow up. We could have had them rolling in the aisles.

This book is therefore dedicated to those aisles.

(Left) Nelson Eddy and Jeanette MacDonald in Girl Of The Golden West

(Below) Oceans Eleven *starring the 'Rat Pack' (l to r) Peter Lawford, Dean Martin, Sammy Davis Jnr and Frank Sinatra*

(Above) Glenda Jackson and George Segal in A Touch Of Class

(Right) Wheeler and Woolsey

Not all teams are created equal.

Then too, not all comedy teams are really teams.

The history of the cinema is littered with pairings of stars and not-so-stars because that helps bring in the public. It's like a two-for-the-price-of-one sale. Nelson Eddy and Jeanette MacDonald . . . Bette Davis and George Brent . . . Fred Astaire and Ginger Rogers . . . A willing public followed them through thick and thin, good and bad and came to know them as more than just a couple of actors working together because somewhere in the Hollywood Hills there is the rent to pay. The rapport between actors who know and like each other has got to be better than the rapport between actors who have just one day met and the next day started reading lines at each other. Friendship is very likely one of the ingredients that goes into the making of a successful team. Just look at the ones which have worked in a film or two . . . Redford and Newman remain great friends . . . Bogart and Bacall were married . . . Tracy and Hepburn might as well have been married . . . Mastroianni and Loren have been fast chums for years . . . Sinatra's "Rat Pack" not only made films together, they also drank and laughed and sang together . . . even the Beatles under the thoroughly expert direction of Richard Lester were turned into a memorable movie team for Hard Day's Night.

In each case a certain kind of magic was there. It was the same kind of magic that Bud Cort and Ruth Gordon found in Harold And Maude . . . the same kind of magic that Glenda Jackson and George Segal found in A Touch Of Class . . . the same kind of magic that happens once or twice when certain actors work together, when all the chemistry is right. A film audience walks away after the final credits and knows that something special has taken place beyond the story of the scriptwriter, beyond the haze and soft focus and close-ups of the camera man, beyond the artful cuts and

10

wipes of the director.

Magic has to be the word because if it could be defined any other way more people would find it more easily.

But the magic of Redford and Newman . . . of Mastroianni and Loren . . . of Tracy and Hepburn . . . is the magic of a film or two . . . three, four at the most. It's something that comes about almost as a side effect to careers that have crossed paths.

The magic of team work is slightly different.

In almost every case, the comedy teams that made it in the movies began their careers on stage or in clubs or on the radio. They developed an act on their way to Hollywood and once they got to town the movies wrapped themselves around the team. Characters and roles were defined. These weren't only actors making movies, these were movies as vehicles for a team. And now the magic that happened was the magic of several minds and several wits all working towards a common goal . . . success of the team.

Like all teams . . . like all single acts . . . failure often came more frequently than success. Sometimes there was only time for a success or two because egos got in the way and the team split up. In other cases entire careers were so strongly linked to team work, that individual careers weren't possible. The end of the team meant the end for everyone in the team. In yet a few other cases, the team worked so well in the beginning that no one knew when to quit. Everyone stayed on too long. And most teams are unfortunately best remembered for their last picture.

Some of the great teams are still great . . . at least in late night re-runs. Some of the minor teams are long forgotten, justifiably so. Some of the laughs are strained, some of the gags were old then and now merit nothing more than a groan. But one thing is certain . . . the comedy teams that rose to stardom in the movies, even if for only fifteen minutes, made it because somewhere before the end of the final reel, the magic was there.

It was there in the late 1920s for Wheeler and Woolsey.

Bert Wheeler was born in 1895, and headlined in vaudeville for many years with his wife Betty. Robert Woolsey was born six years earlier and worked on the so-called legitimate stage, doing everything from light opera with a Gilbert and Sullivan company to playing comedy in *Poppy*, the show which made W. C. Fields a star. It was Flo Ziegfeld who paired Wheeler and Woolsey in his 1928 show *Rio Rita*. And that was the show which got them into the movies. In 1929 Radio Pictures . . . the studio which would eventually become RKO . . . decided to immortalize *Rio Rita*. Wheeler and Woolsey provided the comic relief, by recreating their stage act for the cameras, which happened to have been loaded with Technicolor film. A very big deal in those days.

They made a couple more films immediately following *Rio Rita*, always as comic relief, until 1930 when they were cast in the lead roles of *Half Shot At Sunrise*. "I can't eat this duck," a restaurant customer com-

Olsen and Johnson in Ghost Catcher

plains to Woolsey the waiter, "send for the manager." Woolsey shrugs, "He won't eat it either." And that was one of the funnier jokes!

In all they made 24 films, the majority of which were box-office hits but not necessarily the critics' choice. *Hook, Line and Sinker* features Wheeler saying, "I'm not as big a fool as I used to be," with Woolsey asking, "Did you diet?" In 1931 they did a film called *Girl Crazy*, but the world tends to remember the Mickey Rooney – Judy Garland version that was done ten years later. Betty Grable worked with them in *Hold 'Em Jail*, and then again a few years later in one of Wheeler and Woolsey's better efforts, *The Nitwits*. In between they did a few films which were actually quite funny then and still have some amusing scenes in them today. In *Hips Hips Hooray* they worked with their regular side-kick Dorothy Lee, and the remarkable Thelma Todd. That was followed by *Cockeyed Cavaliers*, again with Dorothy Lee and Thelma Todd, and featuring dialogue such as: Wheeler: "I'm suffering from kleptomania." Woolsey: "Well, take something for it." Wheeler: "I've already taken everything."

With dialogue like that, some of their films had to rely on amusing plots. *Kentucky Kernels* has Wheeler and Woolsey adopting Spanky McFarland then heading down south to fetch Spanky's inheritance. *The Rainmakers* is all about making rain. *High Flyers* had something to do about a jewel theft. It's hard to say exactly what, because by this time the team had run their course and their work was not very funny. The best of their efforts was probably *Cockeyed Cavaliers*. Their partnership ended when Bob Woolsey died in 1938.

It was much the same story for the team of Bobby Clark and Paul McCullough, although their reputation these days is slightly more obscure than Wheeler and Woolsey's. Clark was born in 1888. McCullough was four years older. They met as kids in Springfield, Ohio and, by the time they were teenagers, they had formed a team doing tumbling acts with a travelling minstrel show. Six years later they found themselves working for the Ringling Brothers Circus where they spent more than five years. From there they travelled the world's vaudeville stages, winding up in England as a featured act in the London production of *Chuckles Of 1922*. From there they went to Broadway and by 1928, with star status along the Great White Way, they were hired by the Fox Studios to play in some of the original talkies. They made a series of shorts, decided there wasn't much of a future for themselves in films, and returned to Broadway for several seasons. Then in 1931 RKO talked them back into films. The first comedy short at RKO was *False Rumors*, co-starring James Finlayson who would eventually achieve star-status himself as Laurel and Hardy's silent partner. The highlight of this picture has Clark and McCullough driving a car with a bed attached to the back of it. *The Iceman's Ball* is a custard pie picture. *Melon-Drama* features a bomb planted in a water-melon. While *The Millionaire Cat* is the heart-warming story of a pair of pest exterminators. By the end of 1933 the team started doing

fewer old vaudeville gags and more dialogue related to better story construction. For instance, *Kicking The Crown Around* is the story of an amendment to someone's constitution outlawing salami. But the best of their crop is probably the two-reeler *Odor In The Court* with Clark and McCullough playing the team of divorce lawyers Blackstone and Blodgett whose courtroom antics closely resemble the kind of lunacy you'd expect from the Marx Brothers. It has the same flavour, with dozens of throwaway lines, marching back and forth, and frantic objections to the judge. "I object . . . On what grounds? . . . None . . . Overruled . . . Content!' "

It all ended for them in 1936 when, without any warning, Paul McCullough committed suicide. Today their films are hard to find, most of them buried away under the dust that accumulates on shelves in archives and film studio basements. But for a while, for a handful of comedy shorts, Clark and McCullough were almost as funny as Groucho, Chico and Harpo.

During that same era, Olsen and Johnson were also major vaudeville stars. But they didn't make the trek to Hollywood until later than most teams because vaudeville was where they felt the money was. John Olsen was born in 1892. Harold Johnson was just one year older. Both had musical backgrounds. Olsen was working with a small group when an opening came up for a piano player. Johnson applied for the job. As Olsen liked to explain about Johnson, "He was the first man I ever heard imitate a busy signal on the telephone. I knew I had to have him as a partner." By 1915 both of them had left the band to tour on their own, playing music as a duo, throwing gags in to keep the audiences awake. By 1920 they were stars with their names in lights. Ten years later, with Hollywood anxious to make talkies, Warner Brothers hired Olsen and Johnson for a series of two-reelers that Olsen and Johnson limited to three before leaving Hollywood. They returned to New York for a season of revue work, then toured the country eventually becoming bigger than ever stars in their own show *Hellzapoppin*. While on tour . . . the show took them to the West Coast . . . they made a pair of pictures for Republic. *Country Gentlemen* was first. *All over Town* was second. Neither one offered the future that the *Hellzapoppin* revue did for them, so they went back on the road, eventually to Broadway and a record run of more than 1100 performances. It took the wizards of Hollywood until 1940 to think up the idea that maybe *Hellzapoppin* should be done as a film. It hit the cinemas the follow year. But leave it to Hollywood . . . instead of filming the revue exactly the way the Broadway audiences had seen it, exactly the way the show had earned its reputation as a smash hit, Universal decided to do it their way. They added some kind of plot, which didn't make a lot of sense. Some of the zaniness of the stage version remains, and various well known faces keep popping up. There's Martha Raye as the love interest, and comics like Shemp Howard who was one of the Three Stooges. There is even a cameo appearance of a snow sled named Rosebud.

OW HEAR them on the screen .. funnier than ever!

THE TWO BLACK CROWS

MORAN & MACK

IN

"Why Bring That Up?"

A few years later . . . after doing another successful run with a Broadway show called *Sons O' Fun*, they came back to California for a pair of films called *Crazy House* and *Ghost Catchers* that in their silliness are amusing. *Crazy House* is certainly the better of the two, all the more interesting because it's chock full of cameo guest appearances. Andy Devine. Leo Carillo. Basil Rathbone and Nigel Bruce. Hans Conreid. Count Basie. Shemp Howard, trying at every turn to sell something to Olsen and Johnson, like ovens. And Allan Jones, who at the drop of a hat breaks into *The Donkey Serenade*.

Ghost Catchers, is a lesson in craziness that looks faintly like ghost pictures done before, such as Abbott and Costello's *Hold That Ghost,* and ghost pictures done after, such as Martin and Lewis' *Scared Stiff*. Andy Devine is dressed like a horse. Lon Chaney is dressed like a bear. And if you look very, very fast, supposedly there's even a young Mel Torme dressed like the drummer in the band. "Now don't get the idea that I'm afraid," Johnson says to Olsen when they walk into what is obviously a haunted house. "But then, I didn't believe in radio either."

Their film making days didn't last much longer. Universal decided to put their chips on Abbott and Costello's career, and figured who needed more than one comedy team on the payroll? Olsen and Johnson returned to the stage, worked throughout the '50s and did television whenever they could. At various times they revised *Hellzapoppin*, adapted it for nightclubs, then after more than 45 years in show business, semi-retired. Johnson died in 1962, Olsen three years later.

Because of the nature of vaudeville and burlesque, there was no shortage of comedy teams for the movie moguls to choose from. Not all of them reached anything even close to stardom, however, a few of the minor acts stand out. Smith and Dale, for instance, were already working the New York stages in 1916 with Charlie Dale playing "the only living patient" to Joe Smith's "Dr. Kronkheit". The nurse says to Dale, "Take a chair." Dale says to the nurse, "Wrap it, I'll take it on my way out." When he gets to see the doctor he says, "I'm dubious." Dr. Kronkheit shakes his hand, "Please to meet you Mr. Dubious." Warner Brothers filmed one of their sketches in 1932 as a comedy short and called it *The Heart Of New York*. It's ethnic humour that today might not sit as well with some groups as it did then. Seven years later Smith and Dale did a series of two-reelers for Columbia. But their best film appearance had to come in 1951 when Howard Hughes cast them in his *Two Tickets To Broadway*, asking them to play a pair of delicatessen owners who happen to do some funny old Smith and Dale routines.

Similar, except this time in blackface, were Moran and Mack. Billing themselves as "The Two Black Crows", George Moran and Charlie Mack were both born in Kansas in the late 1880s, and spent their early years in minstrel shows. Their act was based on patter. Moran: "What's an alibi?" Mack: "An alibi is proving that you was where you was when you wasn't so that you wasn't where you was when you was." The first

picture the original Moran and Mack did was in 1929 for Paramount and called *Why Bring That Up?* Then George Moran left the act and was replaced by a fellow named Bert Swor who, billed as Moran, did another film with Charlie Mack for Paramount called *Anybody's War*. Where the first one might have been mildly amusing . . . blackface then was more accepted than it ever would be today . . . the second film was a flop and Paramount let the pair go back to stage work. Radio came along with Amos 'n' Andy, and "The Two Black Crows" faded away. When George Moran reconciled his differences with Charlie Mack, they made another stab at filmwork, this one with Mack Sennett towards the end of his career in a 1932 musical titled *Hypnotized*. It was awful then and is probably worse now. Two years later Charlie Mack was killed in an automobile accident, and while George Moran tried several times to find another Mack, it was all in vain.

As for Amos 'n' Andy, they were fun on radio and actually appeared in the film *The Big Broadcast Of 1936*. But like Moran and Mack, their act was also blackface. It wasn't until the early days of television when black actors started playing the characters that Amos 'n' Andy pioneered regular television employment for black actors in the United States.

Also coming out of radio were Fibber McGee and Molly. Their programme first aired on NBC radio in 1935. Three years later Jim Jordon, who played the lackadaisical Fibber McGee and Marion Jordon, his real-life wife who played Molly, debuted in *This Way, Please* with Betty Grable and Jackie Coogan. It's the best of their film efforts. But their special brand of folksy radio just wouldn't translate to the big screen. Every time they tried the results were fairly depressing. The same thing happened when they made a stab at television. It didn't work. But radio was different and while their Hollywood career was very short-lived, they will always be radio legends.

Not surprisingly, the success of some comedy teams helped bring about the birth of others. In the '40s, Brown and Carney would be brought to Hollywood to see if they could become another Abbott and Costello. You already know what the answer was. They weren't bad, they made a few films as comic relief, but such outings as *Adventures Of A Rookie* were too much of a rip-off of *Buck Privates* and the audiences simply preferred the real thing. Same was true when Tommy Noonan and Peter Marshall teamed up briefly to become another Martin and Lewis. Noonan clowned, Marshall sang, and after three films in ten years they finally got the message.

On the other hand, when Hal Roach saw how successfully Laurel and Hardy were becoming, he decided that there might be room for a female version. He came up with the team of Thelma Todd and ZaSu Pitts and produced seventeen short comedies to prove that they were pretty funny ladies.

A very beautiful woman, Thelma Alice Todd was born in 1905, and was voted Miss Massachusetts in 1924. Two years later she won admission to Paramount's first and only "School of Acting" which the

(Above left) Patsy Kelly
(Above right) ZaSu Pitts
(Above centre) Thelma Todd

studio had hoped would create some new talent. Among her "classmates" was Buddy Rogers. They all debuted together as the "Junior Stars of 1926" in a film called *Fascinating Youth*. After fifteen films in three years, with her career only crawling along, Hal Roach signed her to appear in his comedies. She shows up in Laurel and Hardy's first talkie, *Unaccustomed As We Are*, playing Edgar Kennedy's wife, and has her skirt burned off as she cooks for Laurel and Hardy.

ZaSu Pitts was born in Kansas in 1898, moved with her family to California as a young girl, and knew early on that she was going to be an actress. By 1917 she was working regularly, getting small parts in films such as *A Modern Musketeer* with Douglas Fairbanks Sr. and *Rebecca Of Sunnybrook Farm* with Mary Pickford. By 1931 she was a veteran of some ninety films . . . out of a lifetime total of nearly one hundred and seventy . . . and was very much a star comedienne. Her dramatic talents had been proven in silent masterpieces like *All Quiet On The Western Front*, but for the most part she was known for her work in comedies.

Roach saw the possibilities of pairing ZaSu Pitts with Thelma Todd, and sweetened the pot by allowing them to continue making feature films while turning out these shorts. In the strictest sense of the word, Todd and Pitts were not a comedy team before Roach came along, and even afterwards they were really only talented actors feeding off each other. But they did indeed have a little of that same feel that Laurel and Hardy shared, and even if they didn't reach those same heights, the seventeen short comedies they made together for Roach are kind of funny. Like the Laurel and Hardy characters, the Todd and Pitts roles fit into a formula. Thelma is the smart one and she must somehow untangle the crises that ZaSu innocently brings upon them both. In some of the films, like *Strictly Unreliable* and *Alum and Eve* the girls are put into Laurel and Hardy situations where they have to do some physical comedy. ZaSu gets stuck, Thelma falls in trying to pull her out. That kind of thing. And it doesn't work. In some others, the physical comedy is played down a little, and comes off quite well. In *The Pajama Party*, for example, ZaSu and Thelma find themselves at a very swanky evening where ZaSu has been told to comport herself properly by doing only what the other guests do. At one point some of the guests are wishing someone happy birthday by kicking him in the seat of the pants. The final kick comes from the hostess who shouts, "And one to grow on." Thinking that's the thing to do, ZaSu walks around the party all evening kicking the guests and shouting, "And one to grow on."

The best of the Pitts and Todd partnership were the last five or six films they did together, because by that time Thelma and ZaSu were thinking like a team as well as acting like one. In *Sneak Easily*, ZaSu is a juror who swallows the evidence which just so happens to be a time-bomb about ready to go off. Mayhem reigns in court. *Asleep In The Feet* is a very funny short with Thelma and ZaSu playing taxi dancers. When all the men want to dance with Thelma, leaving ZaSu without customers, Thelma decides to take her friend's career in hand by trying to teach her how to become a sex-symbol. ZaSu of course goes comically overboard at exactly the wrong time . . . just as the man who owns the dance parlour is explaining to the inspectors how respectable he is.

Yet if any one of the films had to be singled out for honours, it would probably be *The Bargain of the Century*. It centres around a huge department store sale where Thelma and ZaSu hope to buy some sheets. On their way they're stopped by a cop, whom they manage to convince to come along to the sale. They figure he'll help them fight off the crowds. But the cop is caught with the girls by one of his superiors and is fired. Because he's out of a job, the girls feel sorry for him and invite him to move in with them until he can find something permanent. That's when they meet Billy Gilbert . . . he was one of the regulars in the series . . . and this time he comes complete with a ridiculous German accent. Mistaken about who he is, the girls think he's a police captain who can get their friend back on the force. They invite him to dinner, during which the out-of-work cop tries to do a magic trick with Gilbert's watch . . . and the watch, in bits and pieces, winds up in the ice cream. Gilbert then goes haywire and wrecks every clock in the apartment.

While Thelma Todd and ZaSu Pitts weren't Laurel and Hardy, it wasn't for their lack of trying.

The seventeen shorts they did together took about two years to make. By 1933, however, ZaSu Pitts was fairly anxious to get back to her feature film career. On the other hand, Thelma Todd felt she had found her niche and wasn't so sure she wanted to quit making short comedies just yet. She started looking for a new partner, and Hal Roach came up with a winner in Patsy Kelly.

Born in 1910 with the name Sarah Veronica Rose Kelly, her parents who were fresh off the boat from County Mayo, Ireland nicknamed her "The Patsy". She took to dance as a young girl, taught her brother how to dance, and he went off in search of a career in show business. He was hired by Frank Fay to work in his vaudeville act, but when Fay met Patsy and saw her dance, he fired the brother and hired her. She worked her way into sketches with Fay, and that won her bigger parts on Broadway, where she spent more than five years in several hit revues. Her reputation as a comedienne couldn't have been more solid when Roach came up with an offer for films. But she was less than impressed. "I never did believe there was a place called Hollywood," she supposedly told her friends. "Somebody made it up." Yet Roach knew what he was doing and talked her into doing *Beauty And The Bus* with Thelma Todd. The girls win a car and promptly proceed to cause an enormous traffic jam. That was followed by *Back To Nature* in which Patsy gives the world a lesson in how not to go camping. In *Air Fright* the girls are stewardesses on a plane loaded with ejection seats. Those three set the pace for the next eighteen films which were shot over the following two years. Where ZaSu Pitts got flustered and waved her arms

The Three Stooges (l to r) Larry Fine, Curly and Moe.

a lot, Patsy Kelly was loud-mouthed and clumsy. Thelma Todd remained the constant, always called upon to save the day. In one film, called *Slightly Static*, the girls share the screen with a group of singing cowboys, one of them being a very young Roy Rogers.

Clowning their way through shorts with titles such as *I'll Be Suing You, Three Chumps Ahead, One Horse Farmers, Bum Voyage* and *All American Toothache* . . . ever-so-subtle Hollywood wanted the audience to know right from the start what they were getting for their money . . . Patsy Kelly and Thelma Todd might well have worked their way up to feature length comedies and become the female Laurel and Hardy team that Roach was looking for. All the elements were there. It would probably only have taken time. But it wasn't on the cards. In December 1935 Thelma Todd was found dead, sitting in the front seat of her car with the engine running. Roach tried fixing Patsy up with another partner . . . first there was a woman named Pert Kelton, then a pair of films with Lyda Roberti . . . but the magic was gone. Patsy went on to feature films. And Hal Roach never found another Laurel and Hardy.

For a while during the '30s there was a pair called Mitchell and Durant . . . they were knock about comics who did pratfalls and slapstick, working for the Fox Studio in films with Alice Faye. But within a few years Frank Mitchell went one way and Jack Durant went another. And anyway, they weren't very good. Then came the Wiere Brothers. And they weren't bad. Harry, Herbert and Sylvester were born in 1908-1909-1910 respectively, in Berlin – Vienna – Prague, also respectively. They were Germany's answer to vaudeville, arriving in Hollywood in 1937 and falling flat on their accents. But they didn't give up. They started touring America, working stage shows and building a minor reputation for themselves in the New World, before returning to Hollywood in the '40s. Although they appeared in films like *Hands Across The Border*, it wasn't until 1947 when they showed up in the Hope-Crosby-Lamour epic *The Road To Rio*, that anyone really took notice. They played three Brazilian street musicians who form a group with Bob and Bing. That film didn't win them any Oscars, but it did keep them working steadily in revues and on television over the next twenty years. Then they returned to Hollywood for their next movie outing. One film in 1947 and a second in 1967 isn't exactly a demanding motion picture career, but going from Crosby and Hope to Elvis Presley must count for something. They worked with

"The King" in *Double Trouble*, playing three detectives hot on Elvis' trail. When Sylvester died in 1970, the Wiere Brothers act came to a close. Although their cinema reputations were decidedly minor, their nightclub and stage work earned them a solid reputation in spite of the fact that stardom alluded them. The main problem with them might have been that they were trying to do slapstick in a world where the ultimate slapstick routines were being done to death by another team. When it comes to pratfalls and clumsiness, hairpulling and eye gouging, no one on earth could ever hope to match the Three Stooges.

With two dozen feature films and nearly 200 short subjects to their credit, the Three Stooges . . . all six of them . . . could never be accused of making a life long trek in search of fresh material. Their act was almost always the same. The gags never seemed to change. Their films were, as Films In Review once summed up, "A minimum of plot and character, a maximum of fast action and sight gags. No sex, no thinking, no complexity, no logic . . . and the ability to turn every situation into a laugh."

It should go without saying that the Three Stooges were not everyone's cup of tea. Sitting through a Three Stooges Retrospective Film Festival for any length of time wouldn't be the easiest of chores. But taken in small doses, and recognizing the fact that as a group they were hard working and dedicated clowns, they certainly deserve their place in film history.

Just which of the Horowitz boys was born first is not very clear. Shemp is generally thought to have been the oldest, but at one point before his death Moe said he was. In any case, Moe's real name was Moses, Shemp was Samuel and Curly, who was definitely the youngest with his birthdate listed as 1903, was Jerome. Another certainty is that by 1909 Moe had left school and was trying to break into show business. They were raised in Brooklyn in an era when that part of New York was producing the comics who would become the backbone of vaudeville. By 1914 Moe had already made a few films, having played very minor roles as a child in long-forgotten one and two reelers, and decided that his future lay as part of a vaudeville act playing Mississippi river boats. When Shemp decided to get into show business a few years later, the two brothers did a blackface act. In the early '20s Moe and Shemp, using Howard as a family name, joined Ted Healy's troupe. He paired them with Larry Fine and called them his Stooges. Fine was born in Philadelphia in 1902 and got into show business as a violin-playing clown. In 1930 they went to Hollywood with Healy to make a feature called *Soup To Nuts*, and when the Stooges found out how badly Healy had cheated them on their paychecks, they went off on their own. The act was called Fine and Howard – Three Lost Souls. Healy tried to make peace with them in 1932 and invited them back to his show, but Shemp refused. He went off to try his luck as a single act, and that brought Curly into the act with Moe and Larry. Shemp made a career out of small parts in films that starred W. C. Fields, Abbott and Costello and even worked in *Hellzapoppin* with Olsen and Johnson. In the meantime, Ted Healy with Moe, Larry and Curly went to Hollywood in 1932 for a string of five films, beginning with *Meet The Baron* that starred Jimmy Durante and Zasu Pitts, *Turn Back The Clock* which featured Mae Clarke, and *Dancing Lady* starring Joan Crawford, Clark Gable, and among others, a newcomer called Fred Astaire. Gable is a Broadway director who is trying to sabotage Joan Crawford's singing audition so he hires the Stooges as musicians. Crawford never stood a chance.

During those same years, the Stooges with Healy hanging on also made a brief series of two-reelers but, by 1934, the association was on the rocks again, and this time they split forever. As soon as Moe, Larry and Curly were on their own, they were approached by both Columbia and Universal to make shorts. They signed with Columbia and stayed there for almost thirty years. The first of their feature films was *The Captain Hates The Sea* which didn't even come close to their best work, like *Woman Haters* and *Men In Black* . . . and that picture was nominated for an Academy Award as Best Short Subject in 1934. It's still a Three Stooges classic.

The basis of their humour was simple. As Moe liked to explain, "People want to laugh with their mouths, not their minds. Audiences want belly-laughs. Rarely will a subtle line or a cute phrase get them into a laughing jag. It takes the old pratfall, a pie in the face, a good chase or a bop on the casaba to keep a laugh going." And he never much cared for the handle slapstick. "Actually we are farcical comedians." Often referred to as "sight comics" . . . because of their use of sight gags . . . Moe who, like most successful clowns, understood certain philosophies of humour, preferred adding the word sound to that . . . making them "sight and sound comics". As he once wrote, "When I belted Curly with a mallet, you heard a cringing, bell-like sound. And when Larry runs a comb through his hair, you hear a crackling sound, like someone had exposed a live-wire."

Their sketches were well planned and always well rehearsed, even if it didn't look like it. They thought carefully about what they were doing and worked hard to make it all come off as being funny. In 1937 one of the motion picture magazines said that the world was divided into two groups. The first thought the Three Stooges were funny. The second wondered why anyone would ever bother laughing. But people did laugh, especially at the two-reelers. They made feature films, mainly as comic relief . . . what else could they be in movies like *My Sister Eileen* which starred Rosalind Russell . . . but the best of their work has to be those shorts. *Hoi Polloi* made in 1935 is often regarded as the best from that vintage, all the more so when compared with their own remake of it in 1947 called *Half-Wits Holiday*. The remake can be funny, but the original is funnier. Anyway, by the time World War II ended, everybody had seen the Three Stooges do their routine, and the gags were wearing thin. *Half-Wits Holiday* marked another point in the group's career because during the shooting of it Curly had a stroke. Shemp was

brought in to replace him. Another short made that same year called *Hold That Lion* also featured Shemp, but Curly made a brief appearance in the film despite his ill-health, and that's the only one that featured all three brothers together.

Shemp stayed on for a while, but he didn't fit into the group the way Curly had. Moe was the boss, Larry was the fall guy and Curly had a wonderful ability to mug faces and get everyone into trouble. The formula was established. Shemp really couldn't find a role that suited the group. The Shemp years were not vintage Stooges. Then, in 1955, Shemp died. The group had just signed another contract with Columbia . . . their 23rd . . . and were to make eight more shorts. Looking around for a new partner, they came up with Joe Besser, whose biggest role had to have been as Stinky, the brat of the Abbott and Costello television series. He was a professional comic with a long track record, but after a few years of lacklustre shorts, Columbia said that's all. In 1958 the Three Stooges decided to pack it all in.

Retirement was very short-lived.

Television discovered the Three Stooges . . . those two-reelers were syndicated across the country . . . and an entire new generation turned on to them. Immediately they were in demand again. This time Moe and Larry went looking for a third team member who came as close as possible to being another Curly. They came up with Joe DeRita, named him Curly Joe, and took off with a Columbia feature called *Have Rocket, Will Travel*.

Now they only made features, many of them with the Three Stooges in some sort of familiar setting. *Snow White and The Three Stooges* was a 1961 effort. The next year they did *The Three Stooges Meet Hercules*. The year after that it was *The Three Stooges In Orbit*. Probably because it's tough to sustain the humour of slapstick in two hour segments, the best of the Three Stooges has to be those two-reelers. On the other hand, during the '60s they did a pair of guest appearances in movies where their routines were kept short and aren't all that bad. They showed up in Frank Sinatra's 1963 film *Four For Texas*, and then again in the movie that featured everybody but Frank Sinatra, *It's A Mad, Mad, Mad, Mad World*. They made their final film in 1965. *The Outlaws Is Coming* turns out to be forgettable, except for the bits and pieces where the Stooges do their thing. As the New York Times wrote about their performance, "Corny, silly, but danged if you don't find yourself laughing, just as you did when you were a kid. Remember?"

With Larry and Moe getting on in years, and Curly Joe no spring chicken himself, their brand of physical mayhem became impossible. So they did the next best thing. They dubbed their own voices on to a series of more than a hundred Three Stooges cartoons that were done for television and as movie house warm-ups.

While making a semi-comeback for television in 1971, Larry suffered a stroke. In 1975 there was some talk of the Stooges appearing in *Blazing Stewardesses* but ill-health forced them to cancel. The Ritz Brothers

got the job. Then Larry died. Four months later Moe passed away.

Not everybody thought the Three Stooges were funny. But they did make some people laugh for more than thirty years, and their two-reelers still show up on television and make more people laugh, so they must have had something going for them. Maybe it was the fact that no one before them, and certainly no one after them, has ever done such good physical comedy . . . or for that matter, so much.

Two groups remain in this chapter of "minor" stars. The first wasn't a team at all, although so many people think of them as one . . . while the second was a wonderful team, stars of radio and television, but for some unknown reason, mere second bananas in the movies.

William Claude Dukenfield was born in Philadelphia in 1890. He often said because of that he's never forgiven the city. Mae West was born in Brooklyn two years later. Each of them had brilliant careers, and each of them on their own was among the greatest comics ever to come out of Hollywood. Their acts were based on looks . . . she had them, he certainly did too, but in another sense . . . sex appeal . . . she had it and he had whatever the opposite of it is . . . and a special delivery of material . . . they both had great style. Neither of them, however, could act. The best thing they could do was be themselves . . . and that they each did brilliantly.

"I never drink anything stronger than gin before breakfast," W.C. used to say. "I have spent forty-six of my sixty-seven years on a diet of olives floating in alcohol. The alcohol to be consumed, the olives to be saved to use over again in alcohol."

She was the woman who made fame and fortune with lines like, "Peel me a grape" . . . and . . . "When I'm good, I'm very good. When I'm bad, I'm better" . . . and . . . "When women go wrong, men go right after them" . . . and, of course . . . "Come on up and see me sometime."

The only time the two did a film together was in 1940 when Universal Pictures matched them in *My Little Chickadee*. She played Flower Belle Lee. He played Cuthbert J. Twillie. And she got top-billing. As a film it's good but hardly anything more than that. As a team effort Fields and West are sensational. The only problem with their future as a team was that they couldn't stand each other. Fields is the snake-oil salesman and card player who is duped into a non-existent marriage with West as a belle of the west. Few scenes in the history of cinema could possibly be as hilarious as their wedding night when she sneaks off to meet her lover and somehow a goat gets into bed, taking her place. When Fields has taken his bath, he gets into bed with the goat thinking it's his bride who has shyly waited for him in her fur coat. But as funny as parts of the film still are, that's how tense some of the times were during the shooting. West didn't drink at all, but knew about Fields' inclinations towards liquid refreshments, and insisted that a clause be drawn into the contract prohibiting him from drinking while working on the film. He countered by referring to her as "My little brood

(l to r) George Burns, Fred Astaire and Gracie Allen in A Damsel In
Distress

mare." When she reworked part of the original script to help her part along, it seemed like a fine idea to her, but not necessarily as fine an idea to Fields. So he tampered with the script to fill out his own part. And she didn't much like that. Her insistence on his sobriety wasn't anything he could have cared for. And the day she found him "on the sauce" she insisted that he be sent home, which couldn't have made anybody very happy. Personal differences notwithstanding, the film somehow got made and in spite of mediocre reviews in 1940, *My Little Chickadee* has to be considered a comic classic. Among other things, it made the team of Mae West and W. C. Fields an indelible image . . . even if it was their only partnership. As she herself put it, "Some people have gotten the quaint idea that I made more than one film with W. C. Fields. No way baby. Once was enough."

The last team might well have deserved a chapter of their own, except that they weren't really movie stars. They are, however, a show business legend.

Nathan Birnbaum was born in New York in 1896. Gracie Ethel Cecile Rosalie Allen was born in San Francisco in 1902. He changed his name to George Burns. She shortened her's to Gracie Allen. And in 1922 . . . each of them having worked their way through vaudeville to Newark, New Jersey . . . they teamed up for a $5 a day booking. Married four years later, Burns and Allen's first big success came in 1929 when they played London's Victoria Palace. Immediately scooped up by BBC Radio, they did twenty-six weeks of on-the-air vaudeville routines. Returning to New York, their star reputation followed them and they found themselves at a Manhatten vaudeville theatre, as close to Broadway as they would ever get. That same year they were asked to pinch hit for Fred Allen . . . no relation to Gracie . . . in a short film being shot on Long Island by Warner Brothers/Vitaphone.

Nobody could possibly describe the film better than George himself has so often done. "They started the camera rolling and Gracie went in and began looking under the ashtrays and in the drawers and I followed her in and said, 'What are you looking for?' She said, 'The audience.' So I said, 'The audience is right there. Right in the camera.' Then I said, 'We're supposed to talk for nine minutes. If we do that we get $1700. Can you talk for nine minutes?' She said, 'Ask me how my brother is.' So I did and she began to talk."

Exactly nine minutes later George looked at his watch. Gracie was in the middle of a joke. He stopped her by announcing, "The nine minutes are up." Then he looked into the camera and told the audience, "We just made $1700." And that was the end of the film. It was called *Lambchops*.

In 1930 Paramount signed them for a series of shorts, the first of which was called *Fit To Be Tied*, and like most of their shorts, it had nothing more to do with cinema that the filming of one of their vaudeville routines. They did a dozen more over the next two years before moving into radio. First they worked for NBC, then they moved to a regular series with ABC, and that's where they originated their famous sign-off.

George would mumble, "Say goodnight Gracie," and she would come back with, "Goodnight Gracie."

Paramount knew a good act when they saw one . . . it was hard not to recognize the talent of Burns and Allen . . . and they signed the couple for *The Big Broadcast of 1932*, one of a series of "all-star" films that let people like Bing Crosby sing on camera. In 1933 they absolutely stole the show when they made *International House*, another all-star production including people like W. C. Fields. Their success got them into *College Humor* starring Bing Corsby. Their part was again to do their vaudeville and radio routines. In their next film *Six Of A Kind*, Burns and Allen actually found themselves with roles that were integrated into the storyline. Charlie Ruggles and Mary Boland are one couple off on a vacation who have invited another couple to come along . . . that's George and Gracie . . . and thanks to them, confusion is the film's comedy theme. W. C. Fields plays the smalltown local sheriff, and the best of his work here is his pool table routine.

The seven films that followed all came quickly . . . and disappeared almost as quickly. *We're Not Dressing* was a Bing Crosby, Carole Lombard, Ethel Merman musical. *Many Happy Returns* starred Guy Lombardo and his orchestra. *Love In Bloom* starred nobody. *Here Comes Cookie* featured such headliners as Cal Norris and Monkey, Jester and Mole, Jack Cavanaugh and Partner, Seymour and Corncob, Moro and Yaconelli, and the Six Candreva Brothers, to name only a few. Then came *The Big Broadcasts* of 1936 and 1937, and *College Holiday* with Jack Benny and Martha Raye. It wasn't until 1937 that they made their best feature, *A Damsel In Distress*.

Starring Fred Astaire and Joan Fontaine, this was Astaire's first dancing musical without Ginger Rogers since 1933. The film is generally remembered for such hit songs as *A Foggy Day In London Town* and *Nice Work If You Can Get It*. But anyone who loves comedy has to remember the film for Burns and Allen. They play Astaire's friends and public relations persons. Some of their lines are classics and straight out of the Burns and Allen joke book. For instance, she asks him what the date is and he tells her to look at the date on the newspaper sitting nearby. She says that won't do because, "It's yesterday's paper." George and Gracie easily hold their own when it comes to dancing with Astaire. And watching *A Damsel In Distress* these days is such fun that it seems a shame no one thought of teaming Burns and Allen with Astaire more than once.

Their last two films were *College Swing*, a Raoul Walsh epic that had a cast of thousands, including Bob Hope, Martha Raye, Edward Everett Horton, Ben Blue, Betty Grable, et al. and *Honolulu*, an MGM venture with Eleanor Powell and Robert Young. On her own, Gracie made three films between 1939-1944 but none of them went very far. Certainly nowhere near as far as George went in his solo film career after Gracie's death starring in such wonderful movies as *The Sunshine Boys* and *Oh God*.

As a team their real success came first on radio, and then during all those years when they transformed their radio routines on to a weekly television series. Gracie Allen died in 1964. "I never would have been a star without Gracie," George has often admitted. And once the comedy team of Burns and Allen was over, someone in an epitaph to Gracie put it very simply. The man was a radio commentator who on the day of Gracie's funeral said goodbye to her with "More people have left less of a legacy than you."

Lucky for us, their reruns live on.

Burns & Allen in College Humor

Laurel + Hardy

No one planned the partnership.

It just sort of happened.

And even then, in the beginning when those first few silent films were in the can, no one guessed what those two would eventually become. Hollywood didn't always know what made America laugh. Although the fat one and the skinny one seemed to. They were funny. Perhaps eventually the funniest of all. But at least in the beginning no one, not even the two of them, knew just how funny they could be.

Stan was born Arthur Stanley Jefferson in Lancashire, England in 1890. He was the son of a small time actor and an equally small time singer. In 1907, Arthur decided to try his hand at acting, called himself Stan Jefferson, and spent the next few years touring Great Britain, at times sharing a stage with a then little-known comic named Charlie Chaplin. In 1910, when he came to the United States for the first time, Stan Jefferson was Chaplin's understudy. Two years later, returning to America to work the vaudeville circuit, part of Stan's act was a Chaplin imitation.

He bounced around the country until about 1916 when he joined forces with an Australian singer called Mae Dahlberg who supposedly convinced him to change his name. She felt that any name spelled with thirteen letters was unlucky so she suggested Laurel. He agreed and they billed themselves as Stan and Mae Laurel.

It was during the following year while playing in New York, that Stan made his film debut in a one reeler titled *Nuts In May*. The plot was simple: Stan escapes from a mental institution wearing a three-cornered Napoleon hat. When Carl Laemmle Sr., the boss at the Universal Studios saw it, he thought Stan would be the perfect actor in a series of comic shorts based on a popular character of the day known as Hickory Hiram. However, Laemmle guessed wrong. The series never caught on and Stan quickly retreated back to vaudeville. Yet films were an easy way of paying bills when he was in between bookings so he made the odd short now and then, one of them being a two-reeler for Metro called *Lucky Dog*. He played the good guy pitted against the villain whose first title cards to Stan read "Put 'em up insect before I comb your hair with lead." Nine years later Stan couldn't even remember that the villain in question was a southern actor named Oliver Norvell Hardy.

Over those next nine years Stan made a name for himself as a vaudevillian, and also racked up some seventy one- and two-reelers. As they were all silent films, they relied heavily on his mime technique, which in some ways closely rivalled that of his old chum, Chaplin. But, after a while, Stan began to think that perhaps his real future was behind the cameras. He could write gags and he was interested in directing, and by 1926 he was employed at the Hal Roach Studios as a producer/director/writer. And directing comedy was probably the only thing he had in mind when he started work on a film called *Get 'Em Young*.

Oliver Norvell Hardy was born in 1892 in the genteel southern town of Harlem, Georgia. He was named after his father and his middle name came from his mother's maiden name, but for most of his life his friends simply called him Babe.

Even as a child he had a weight problem and the cruelty he suffered from other children affected his schoolwork. But he could sing and make people laugh, and as a child he spent time touring the south in a Minstrel show. By the time he was twenty-one, he decided he wanted to become a movie star, so he went to Jacksonville, Florida and auditioned for the Lubin Studios who hired him. Invariably he was cast as a comic heavy. *Outwitting Dad* is generally said to be his first film, although there is some doubt. It was a long time ago and he made dozens of films there, almost everyone of them long forgotten. Three years of steady film work later . . . at the rate of $5 per day, guaranteed three days a week . . . he went to New York to do a string of films there, before returning for another series of shorts with Lubin. He supplemented his income by singing in nightclubs, did another stint of making movies in New York then headed for Hollywood. It was 1918. Babe Hardy was a veteran of at least one hundred films, including some of the famous Billy West comedies. In California, over the next eight years, he worked at various studios, among them Vitagraph, before joining Hal Roach's company. In 1925 Babe even played the *Tin Woodman* in a version of *The Wizard Of Oz*. By the time Roach cast him to play the butler in *Get 'Em Young*, Babe Hardy had already worked in two hundred films.

The day before shooting was to begin, Babe burned his arm in a cooking accident. No one else could be dredged up to play his part, so Roach appealed to Stan Laurel to fill in. Stan refused until Roach came up with more money. He then took the part and invented his "whimpering cry". As the story goes, there was a moment when the camera focused on him, he couldn't think of any business to do so he started to weep. It got a laugh from the crew on the set although it seems Stan didn't like it all that much. He knew it was funny but he didn't have any intention of ever using it again. As far as he was concerned, this sudden return to acting was a one-shot deal. But Roach had other ideas the moment he saw the film. He offered Stan more money yet again to write himself into the next project, *Slipping Wives*. Babe Hardy came back to work and, for the second time in their careers, they shared a sound stage.

During the years 1926-1927, Stan Laurel and Babe Hardy made some twenty films together. The order in which the films were shot was not always the order in which they were released, so it's nearly impossible these days to date them accurately. However, those very early efforts include some minor classics such as *Duck Soup, Why Girls Love Sailors* and *Do Detectives Think?* In the latter, Laurel and Hardy play a pair of bumbling detectives who are hired to protect a judge from a killer he's sent to prison but who has escaped to seek revenge. The judge is played by James Finlayson, an important ingredient in dozens of Laurel and Hardy films. Known around Hollywood as Finn, he was born in Scotland in 1887 and had worked on the English

stage before coming to the United States in 1911. After making a reputation for himself on Broadway, he went to California in 1916 where he eventually found work as one of Sennett's Keystone Cops. From there Hal Roach hired him, cast him in some Our Gang comedies and, even gave him a few leading parts in comic shorts. Finn, however, never attained stardom. Famous for his ability to do a double-take, instead he became the perfect foil for Stan and Ollie. And a good measure of their early success is due to his ability to help them get laughs. He slowed down in his later years but never stopped working until his death in 1953.

Do Detectives Think? opens with the title card reading, "The defendant had killed two Chinamen, both seriously." A few shots later the title card tells you, "The judge had married for love. Nobody ever figured out what his wife had married for." Finn pulls off a wonderful piece of business when the killer comes looking for him while he's in the bath. The killer stalks into the bathroom, Finn submerges. The killer turns his back to the tub, Finn comes up for air. The killer swings around, Finn dives underwater. It's very funny. But the best part of the film is a few minutes of brilliant pantomime by Stan and Babe, proving that they were more than just two actors working together on a film. Even if they weren't officially thought of by anyone as a team when they first started, by 1926 they were already thinking like one.

The two detectives are on their way to the judge's house. The moon is full, casting long shadows as they pass the entrance to a cemetery. The wind picks up and blows their hats into the graveyard. Ollie sends Stan in to get the hats but, as he passes a wall at the far end of the cemetery he spots his own shadow, thinks it's a ghost and panics. On successive attempts to fetch the hats, separately or together, the "ghost" is always there. Neither Stan nor Ollie can sneak up on it, crawl past it or run fast enough to get by it. It takes them a long time to finally retrieve their hats and go on their way. The gag is well woven into the story although it has nothing at all to do with the plot. The only reason it's there is to get laughs.

Part of the Hal Roach formula for comedy was based on the idea that a film had to be "clocked". The average two-reeler had to have a set number of laughs, perhaps as many as seventy-five, and when the films were shown to a preview audience, someone actually sat there counting how many times the audience laughed. If it "clocked" less than the required number then something was wrong and gags were either added or the film was re-edited. The results were good short comedies produced by Roach at the rate of one a week. When it became evident that the fat Ollie and the skinny Stan were more than just two actors who could get laughs together, Roach gave them more opportunities to develop their characters. He cast them first as bit players, then as stars playing roles, finally as Stan and Ollie with plots and gags built around them. Because production schedules were so hectic in those days, and records from them nearly non-existent, there is some doubt as to which was the very first "Laurel and Hardy" film.

Many people credit *Putting The Pants On Philip*, even though it was released after *Let George Do It* and *The Battle Of The Century*. Most people tend to agree, however, that it was during the making of these three films that Stan and Ollie found themselves knitted together as a team. In *Putting The Pants On Philip*, they did not play themselves. Babe was cast as the Honorable Piedmont Mumblethumber and Stan as his nephew Philip, just off the boat from Scotland in a kilt (which explains the title). At one point Philip is standing on a grating when a gust of air blows his kilts up, predating Marilyn Monroe and *The Seven Year Itch* by decades. Later, Philip takes a little snuff, then sneezes so heavily that his underpants fall down. Finally, when a woman wants to cross a muddied curb, Philip with underpants back in place, gallantly lays down his kilt like Raleigh's cape. The woman crosses. The Hon. P. Mumblethumber also insists on crossing with the kilt, and he immediately sinks into six feet of mud. Suffice it to say that this was not the most sophisticated of comedies but the film did allow Stan and Babe to play the sort of Laurel and Hardy characters that would make them famous.

The same is true for *The Battle Of The Century*, which contains the world's greatest pie fight.

A joke already over-used by 1927, Stan Laurel decided to take the "pie in the face" gag to the very limit. As the team's chief gag writer . . . Babe preferred to play golf . . . Stan helped to build a believable plot around a pie fight to end all pie fights. Ollie has taken an insurance policy out on Stan and to collect, he's trying to get Stan to slip on a banana peel. Stan unwittingly misses it every time. But a man delivering custard pies doesn't. He steps on it and falls, blaming Ollie and therefore instigating a pie fight. It builds slowly, eventually getting to the point where everyone in the scene is throwing pies back and forth. To prove it was "the last word" in pie fights, they not only bought real custard and cream pies for the film, but managed to splatter a reported four thousand of them!

The banana peel/custard pie routine was used differently in *From Soup To Nuts* just a year later. Stan and Ollie are waiters hired for a private party. The script called for Ollie to come into the room carrying a huge pie, slip on a banana peel, and land face down in the pie. But one of the reasons Laurel and Hardy are so special is that they understood the concept of establishing logic with the gag. A banana peel appearing out of nowhere would render the joke ridiculous. To accomplish credibility, they plant a dog in the scene who eats the banana then leaves the peel in the centre of the room.

Of course, a banana peel is almost a cliché. You see it and immediately think someone is about to trip. The instant that Ollie appears with the pie, the gag is signalled. But again, Laurel and Hardy and their writers understood how to play a gag. Ollie doesn't simply arrive with the pie. First he goes through a series of very smug explanations to Stan, suggesting that only Oliver Norvell Hardy could properly serve such a pie. Building up conceit builds up the laugh, even if the

joke is signalled. That build-up is very slow, making the audience wait for the joke. When it finally happens there is almost a sense of relief, which is translated into laughter. Then, to get the most out of the gag, Ollie does his "slow burn" by lying perfectly still, face down in the pie.

Because everything leading up to the gag is logical, nothing gets in the way of the punch-line. Another good example of this technique is "the crab in the seat of the trousers" routine from the 1929 short, *Liberty*. Stan and Ollie escape from prison and go through a bunch of gags where they try to put civilian clothes on top of their prison garb. Naturally they keep winding up with each other's clothes. Every time they make an exchange . . . with Ollie's best annoyed expression and Stan's most bewildered look . . . they mix up the exchange so in the end no exchange really takes place. At one point in *Liberty* this happens near a fish market where there are a couple of crates of live crabs. One falls into the seat of Ollie's slacks just as he's pulling them on. That's funny, but as he starts to walk away, nothing happens to show that he knows the crab is there. The audience can see the joke is on its way but Laurel and Hardy deliberately wait for those expectations to build up. In fact, nothing happens with the crab at all until Stan and Ollie are on the top of a very high building, trying to walk along the edge of a construction beam. That's when the crab strikes.

Call it "the fun of expectation". And there aren't too many comics who ever used it to better effect than Laurel and Hardy. It is the basis for a lot of the best jokes in their masterpiece, *The Perfect Day*.

Dated 1929 and directed by James Parrott . . . the man who directed many of their best shorts . . . Stan and Ollie are taking their wives and Ollie's father-in-law for a drive and a picnic. The father-in-law, played by Edgar Kennedy who was another regular face in their films, sports a huge bandage on one foot, the kind worn by people suffering from gout. The minute you see it you know exactly what's going to happen. What you don't know is when. And that's Laurel and Hardy's trump card. They make you wait.

The film opens with all of them trying to climb into the car. Once that's done, the car blows a tyre which means everyone's now got to get out. Ollie decides he will change the tyre, so he takes off his jacket while the old man with the bandaged foot sits on the running board. Ollie asks Stan for the tyre iron. He fetches it from the back seat, steps out to hand it to Ollie and promptly crushes the old man's bandaged foot. The old man howls and the gag is done. But they've set it up to be done again and this time they catch you unaware. As Ollie grabs the tyre iron from Stan, it accidentally drops out of both of their hands and crashes on to the old man's foot. He howls a second time. Stan picks up the tyre iron but Ollie is furious and takes it from Stan who loses his balance, falls backwards, and lands you know where. The old man howls for a third time. Finally the tyre iron falls under the car and Stan goes to retrieve it, inadvertently slamming the car door on the bandaged foot, bringing four howls from the old man,

and four laughs out of the same gag.

When you look closely at their films, especially the shorts, and think of them as a series of logical progressions of gags, you can see how simple they kept the plots. It's one of the key elements of their success but at the same time one of the major factors of their inability to make feature length films. Few shorts could be funnier than *Big Business*, yet few plots could be simpler. There's almost no plot at all. Laurel and Hardy are Christmas tree salesmen in the middle of summer. It's a near-perfect comedy in every sense, pitting the two of them against the man who doesn't want to buy a tree – Finlayson.

They arrive at Finn's door and Ollie offers to demonstrate his "hard sell" approach. Finn refuses to buy a tree and slams the door in Ollie's face. Unfortunately, part of the tree he's trying to sell is caught in the door. He rings the bell, freeing the tree when Finlayson opens the door but catching Stan's coat in it when Finlayson shuts the door. This gag runs back and forth until Finn gets annoyed, grabs the tree and tosses it away. Ollie mumbles, "I don't think he wants a tree," but Stan who has been thinking about all of this rings Finn's bell to ask, "Could I take your order for next year?"

Finn comes out of his house with a huge pair of shrub cutters, goes to the tree and snips it into pieces. Looking at each other, Stan and Ollie declare war. Stan carves up Finn's front door while Ollie pulls Finn's ear. Retaliating, Finn takes Ollie's watch, checks the time, then smashes it. Within seconds, all hell has broken loose. This "reciprocal destruction" is watched by Finn's neighbours and a cop on the beat. Stan and Ollie completely wreck Finn's house, while he systematically rips their car to shreds. When the cop finally asks who started all of this, Ollie fiddles with his tie and Stan starts to cry. Instantly, everyone else is crying too. To make friends with Finn, Stan offers him a cigar. Naturally, it explodes just as Stan and Ollie make their hasty exit.

Even today that film is funny. But it probably only works because everyone involved with it understood how delicately balanced this "reciprocal destruction" gag had to be. Missing that balance would have put Stan and Ollie and Finn in the category of the Three Stooges. To avoid slapstick, Laurel and Hardy must not come across as being the nastiest and most spiteful guys in town. It's only funny if the audience sympathises with them. And that's done by playing off Stan and Ollie's natural sense of ineptitude, in contrast to Finn's quick temper and rudeness. Even if Stan and Ollie in this film are spiteful and nasty, they get away with it because Finlayson is more spiteful and nastier.

By the time *Big Business* came around, sound films were the big business in Hollywood, and the timing couldn't have been better for Stan and Babe. For a lot of other silent stars, the timing couldn't have been worse. Either their voice was wrong or they couldn't read lines. Some people simply didn't translate into sound. Turpin, Blue, Lloyd, Keaton, even Chaplin. His screen image was based on mime and the moment

(Overleaf) Stan's original ambition was to work the other side of the camera. Here he gets his wish in a twee publicity shot

he started to speak, the character started to change. Not so with Laurel and Hardy. First of all, their voices were pleasant and that enhanced their appeal. Then they understood that they didn't necessarily have to become comedians who depended on spoken gags for laughs, they could make sound complementary to their well executed mime. As Stan Laurel has been quoted, "We decided we weren't talking comedians and of course preferred to do pantomime, like in our silents. So we said as little as possible, only what was necessary to motivate the things we were doing."

No other film they did displays their understanding of sound as well as the 1932 three-reeler that earned them their only Academy Award, *The Music Box*. Their job is to deliver a piano to a house at the top of a long and narrow set of steps. Ollie is the boss, and naturally he's one hundred per cent certain that he and Stan can get the piano up the steps. It's a sound film, done mostly in mime, with Stan and Ollie ineptly trying to move the piano. Once they finally get the piano to the front door of the house, a second set of gags is put into motion. The mailman informs them that the easiest way to deliver anything to the house is by the road at the rear. With a pronounced, "Why didn't we think of that before," from Ollie, they take the piano back down the steps, put it on the van and drive it around to the house. Then they shift into third gear, now faced with the problem of how to get the piano into the house. The front door is locked, so Ollie devises a way to get it in through the second floor window. They somehow manage that, bring the piano down the staircase and place it in the living room. They have just enough time to do a brief bit of song and dance before the owner of the house comes home and in a rage, points out that they have totally wrecked the place.

By very carefully and skilfully mixing dialogue with mime, they managed to make themselves stars during this delicate point of transition from silents to talkies. They used dialogue to set up their mime routines, and used mime . . . especially mugging . . . to punch up their spoken lines. Ollie's tie twiddle and Stan's whimpering cry. Ollie's long camera stare and Stan's bewildered eyebrow-raised head scratch. They actually mugged their way into the sound era.

When they played with language, they did it with their usual flare. Brought before a judge on a vagrancy charge, they're asked how they plead. Ollie says confidently, "Not guilty." The judge wonders, "On what grounds?" And Stan responds with his sincerest expression, "We weren't on the ground. We were sleeping on a park bench."

A lot of their dialogue was based on slightly familiar vaudeville gags, although they certainly relied less on that than a lot of other comics in films. In *Men Of War* they play a pair of sailors who meet two girls at a soda fountain. Ollie wants to offer them a soda but he and Stan only have fifteen cents, enough for just three sodas. So Ollie tells Stan, "When I ask you to have a drink, you refuse." The very same routine shows up years later in the Abbott and Costello film *Keep 'Em Flying* but, where Bud and Lou can only afford one

sandwich and play the gag for the lines, Stan and Ollie make much more use out of the mime that goes with the dialogue. Convinced that Stan understands, Ollie asks the girls what they want, and they say sodas. Ollie orders the third soda, then turns to Stan, who also orders a soda. Ollie glares at him, politely excuses himself to the girls and says in an aside to Stan, "Don't you understand? We've only got fifteen cents. Now when I ask you to have a drink, you refuse. Do you understand?" Stan nods that he does. Ollie asks everyone again what they want to drink. The girls say sodas, he says he'll have a soda, and so does Stan.

"Just a moment please," Ollie says with all of his southern charm. "Pardon me once more." He turns slowly to Stan and very deliberately says, "Can't you grasp the situation? You've got to refuse."

Stan looks at him. "But you keep asking me?"

Ollie tells him, "But we're only putting it on for the girls."

Now it seems as if Stan comprehends, so Ollie again takes the orders. This time when he asks Stan what he'll have, Stan smiles proudly to show that he does understand, "I don't want anything." Satisfied, Ollie has a content smile on his face, when one of the girls insists that Stan have something. "All right," Stan now says, "I'll have a banana split."

Played side by side with the Abbott and Costello version of the same gag, you not only see how broad Abbott and Costello were but also how slowly paced Laurel and Hardy were. It's extraordinarily slow. But that pace loaned itself extremely well to the balance of dialogue and mime that Laurel and Hardy worked with in their short films. They never punch at their lines. Instead they seem as if they're simply coming up with each line, one by one. In *The Private Life Of Oliver VIII*, there's a short bit of dialogue where Ollie has persuaded Stan to stay awake and keep guard as Ollie is the planned victim of a murderess. Ollie falls asleep and a few minutes later, so does Stan. When Ollie wakes up suddenly to find his bodyguard asleep, he shakes Stan awake with, "What are you trying to do? Do you want me to get my throat cut?"

Stan answers meekly, "No".

"Well then," says Ollie, "don't go to sleep."

As if it actually made sense, Stan replies, 'Well, I can't tell when I'm asleep."

"That's why I want you to stay awake," Ollie says, making that obvious. "So you can see that you're not asleep."

Now Stan feels he must explain. "Well I couldn't help it." He pleads with Ollie, "I was dreaming I was awake. And then I woke up and found myself asleep".

It just isn't the kind of stuff that radio programmes were made of in those days. There is no real joke that gets tagged with a final line followed by a long pause when the audience is supposed to laugh. It's dialogue wrapped up in mime and, while the pantomime worked alone in their silent films, their dialogue was designed to work better combined with mime.

Take *Twice Two*, a 1933 film directed by James Parrott. Stan is married to the former Miss Hardy,

played by Babe. And Ollie is married to the former Miss Laurel, played by Stan. The split-screen technique that Parrott used is wonderful. The plot that Stan Laurel and the studios writers came up with is no more complicated than this: the two boys come home to a house they share with their wives for an anniversary dinner. At one point Stan is sent out with some money to buy ice cream, but the candy store where he goes doesn't have his first choice of flavour, so he spends one of his nickels calling back to the house asking everyone's second choice. The candy store owner doesn't have that one either so Stan spends another nickel calling home. Of course, he eventually runs out of money to buy ice cream, and when he does the candy store owner tells Stan that ice cream isn't even sold at the candy store but at the ice cream parlour next door. So much for the sub-plot and the joke-filled dialogue.

The thing that's significant about the film is that there is a one or two minute spot of pure Stan Laurel pantomime that is absolutely classic. He's sitting at the table next to his wife, and is served soup. Without one word being spoken, and with the same stationary camera shot, Stan tucks his napkin in at his chin, lifts his spoon to drink his soup, and ends up with a spoonful of napkin. Slightly perplexed, he tries it again, only to get the napkin again. He then goes about trying to rearrange the napkin round his neck so that he can get a spoon to his mouth without winding up with the napkin. It's sheer magic.

It's also something else. Something a lot more subtle. It's a way of reinforcing the childlike ineptitude of the character. And this is yet another area where Laurel and Hardy understood that by delicately combining dialogue with mime, they could so richly paint a character's portrait that he would end up as real as the actor playing the role.

"I am Mr. Hardy, Oliver Norvell Hardy, and this is my friend, Mr. Laurel." Always Mister. It gave them both a sense of dignity, and Ollie especially, a feeling of urbanity. In fact, writes Leonard Maltin in his excellent portrait of them, Laurel and Hardy, "Created characters who are so utterly believable that it was difficult to picture them being any different off-screen. This credibility was supported by the men's decision to use their real names on-screen, enabling people around the world to feel as if they actually knew Stan Laurel and Oliver Hardy."

Adding to that, John McCabe, who has written several books about the team and in many ways is their official biographer, feels that by the time they established themselves in sound comedies, they had firmly gelled their on-screen characters into a permanent form, being, "Two supremely brainless men, totally innocent of heart and almost outrageously optimistic." He says that their bowler hats, for instance, crowned their essential dignity and that the way they used and misused those hats were outward signs of their fight to maintain that dignity. Then came the gestures and phrases that were their trademarks. He cites the way Laurel folded his arms, the way he walked so flat-footedly, his whimpering cry, the way he blinked his eyes, and the way he scratched his head. As for Hardy, the basic gestures became the way he extended his pinky when he tipped his hat, the way he fiddled with his tie, the way he would point his finger at Stan when he wanted Stan to remove his hat, and the way he would stare right into the camera to show his own exasperation.

"The two characters are the definition of friendship," McCabe goes on, "living in a life framework of hopes perpetually deferred yet hourly renewed; the ultimate optimists. 'Why don't you do something to help me?' Ollie asks Stan, who does, pushing them both therewith into new catastrophe. The Hardy lament which most characteristically identified the team's essence is, 'Here's another fine mess you've gotten me into!' Those messes delighted millions, particularly during the Depression years when the troubles of the day were diminished by empathising with the troubles of these two lovable dimwits and their everyday frustrations writ large."

Oliver Hardy himself saw it a bit differently. "Once in a while someone will ask me when Stan and I dreamed up the characters we play in the movies. They seem to think these two characters aren't like anyone else. I know they're dumber than anyone else, but there are plenty of Laurel and Hardy's in the world."

The short comedies now seem to have been the true "Golden Age" of Laurel and Hardy, and looking back, it's as if the beginning of the end came as they switched from short films to features.

But then, it doesn't seem that the switch was their idea.

Somewhere towards the end of 1932, Hal Roach decided the real money to be made with Laurel and Hardy was in features. His distributor, MGM, agreed. Years later, Stan Laurel in an interview explained that he and Ollie were not of the same conviction. "We should have stayed in the short film category. There is just so much comedy one can do along a certain line and then it gets to be unfunny." Eventually he added, "We didn't want to do feature films in the first place, and even though I've got some favourites among them, I'm sorry we ever did go beyond the two and three reelers."

They did a total of 27 features, and people like John McCabe say that only a handful are really worth seeing today. He lists, for example, *Swiss Miss*, *Blockheads*, *A Chump At Oxford* and *Saps At Sea*. Certainly one that should be on the list is *Sons Of The Desert*. It's the story of Laurel and Hardy as members of a fraternal organization, the Sons of the Desert, one of those semi-secret clubs where grown men wear silly hats. The film opens with Laurel and Hardy arriving late to a meeting, creating something of a disturbance as they try to locate their seats. The main topic of discussion at that meeting is to convince the local members to attend the national convention in Chicago. When everyone stands to pledge their allegiance to the club, Stan starts to cry because he is afraid his wife won't let him go. Ollie assures him that he can arrange everything. Most of that scene is mime, again pointing out that Laurel and Hardy continued to feel that they were at their best when left alone.

Because women in Laurel and Hardy films were always bossy and overpowering, a sexist attitude viewed by some women today as being a serious fault with these films, their wives refuse to let them go. So Ollie cooks up a scheme where he pretends to be ill. Stans brings in a quack doctor who prescribes for Ollie a trip to Hawaii. Because his health is at stake, Ollie's wife insists he follow the doctor's orders. Ollie then announces, referring to Stan, "If I'm going to Honolulu alone, he's going with me."

Instead of Hawaii, they head for Chicago. While they're frolicking at the convention, the ship they're supposed to be on starts to sink. The passengers are rescued and returned to California. When Stan and Ollie don't show up with the other passengers, their wives become anxious. Consoling each other, they decide to take in a movie. The newsreel playing at the theatre that night is about the national convention of the Sons Of The Desert. And guess whose faces show up on the film. When Stan and Ollie finally come home, their wives berate them like two spoiled children. Stan cries. Ollie fiddles with his tie, and comments, "Nice little mess you've gotten me into."

Sons Of The Desert managed to take so many of the successful elements of the short comedies and stretch them into a feature. Unfortunately, from 1934 to 1940, their successes diminished because the more they tried to stretch their comedy into that longer format, the thinner it got. They eventually left the Roach Studio and spent the next five years wandering around Hollywood, from studio to studio, until they officially retired from films in 1945.

The slight story line and heavy reliance on mime worked brilliantly in their two- and three-reelers. Their slow pace was perfect for fifteen minute film. It simply didn't translate into seven or eight reels. Sure there are bits and pieces of their features which are wonderful. If you look very, very closely at some of them you find in-jokes. In *A Chump At Oxford* they play a scene in front of a bank called The Finlayson National Bank. In *Way Out West* there is a scene where Ollie walks into a room to change clothes, and in almost the next frame he comes out fully dressed. Stan actually asks, "How did you get dressed so quickly?" And Ollie responds, "Never you mind." *Babes In Toyland* is a favourite with kids but as a film for adults, it just doesn't work. *Swiss Miss* might have been one of the better ones, but it was edited so badly that some parts of it don't make sense at all. Put frankly, most of their features are just too uneven.

"You've got to settle for a simple basic story in our case," Stan once told an interviewer, "and then work out all the comedy that's there and then let it alone. But you can't take a whole, long series of things we do and stick them all together in eight reels, and expect to get a well balanced picture out of it."

One feature that absolutely must be seen by any serious student of the art is *Pardon Us*, one of their very first features. But don't see it in English. Try to catch it in French, German, Spanish or Italian. The foreign markets were already open to them in 1931-1932 so they dubbed a handful of shorts and this one feature into different languages, and Stan and Ollie did it themselves. They would do each scene five times, once in English, then once in each of the other four languages. Because they only understood English, they had no idea what they were actually saying to each other. Their lines were written out phonetically on cue cards off camera. For each version they also had a language coach, but that didn't make their attempt at being polyglots any less funny.

That foreign markets demanded their films should have been a clue as to just how famous they were. But during their heyday, especially the early '30s, it seems they never realised how popular they had become. Roach kept them under separate contract, which tightly bound them to the studio. By the time they broke away their stars were fading. Yet even at their peak they were still never as popular as they seem to be today, which says a great deal about the timelessness of their comedy. Certainly in those days they didn't enjoy all the trappings of stardom. Abbott and Costello were reportedly each earning $10,000 a week plus percentages at Universal. Roach paid Laurel and Hardy about a third of that, without any percentages.

As a team they made one hundred and four short and feature length films, although the figure varies a bit depending on who's counting. In three instances Babe Hardy worked without Stan Laurel. He did a 1939 films called *Zenobia*, a 1949 epic with John Wayne called *The Fighting Kentuckian,* and a 1950 picture with Bing Crosby called *Riding High*. In 1951 Babe and Stan made their final film together. It's called *Atoll K* and is well worth missing. But it did renew their partnership and the following year they went to England on a nine month tour of music halls, playing every night to packed audiences. It was such a success that they repeated the tour in 1953. They might have found a new life for themselves on stage except that Babe's health started to deteriorate. He died in 1957. Stan passed away eight years later.

"Basically," Hal Roach was known to have said, "the Stan and Ollie characters were childlike, innocent. The best visual comedians imitate children really. No one could do this as well as Laurel and Hardy and still be believable. We always strived for that, and we sure must have succeeded, because the world is still laughing at them."

Indeed . . . they were very funny.

The Films of Laurel and Hardy

75 Short Films

All done at the Hal Roach Studios

Slipping Wives – 1926
Putting The Pants On Philip
The Battle Of The Century – 1927
Let George Do It
The Second Hundred Years
With Love And Hisses
Sailors Beware
Do Detectives Think?
Flying Elephants
Sugar Daddies
Call Of The Cuckoo
The Rap
Duck Soup
Eve's Love Letters
Love 'Em And Weep
Why Girls Love Sailors
Hats Off
Leave 'Em Laughing – 1928
From Soup To Nuts
You're Darn Tootin'
Their Purple Moment
Should Married Men Go Home?
Habeas Corpus

Two Tars
We Faw Down
The Finishing Touch
Early to Bed
Liberty – 1929
Unaccustomed As We Are
 (their first sound film)
Double Whoopee
Big Business
Men O' War
Wrong Again
That's My Wife
Berth Marks
Bacon Grabbers
Angora Love
The Perfect Day
They Go Boom
The Hoosegow
Night Owls – 1930
Blotto
Be Big
Brats
Below Zero
The Laurel and Hardy Murder Case
Another Fine Mess
Hog Wild
Chickens Come Home – 1931

Laughing Gravy
Our Wife
Come Clean
One Good Turn
Helpmates
Beau Chumps
Any Old Port – 1932
The Music Box
County Hospital
The Chimp
Scram
Their First Mistake
Towed In A Hole – 1933
Twice Two
Me and My Pal
The Midnight Patrol
Dirty Work
Busy Bodies
Going Bye Bye – 1934
The Private Life of Oliver VIII
Them Thar Hills
The Live Ghost
Tit for Tat – 1935
The Fixer-Uppers
Thicker Than Water
Tree In A Test Tube – 1943
 (made for the US Government)

23 Features

Pardon Us – 1931 – Hal Roach
Pack Up Your Troubles – 1932 – Hal Roach
Fra Diavolo – 1933 – Hal Roach
Sons Of The Desert – 1933 – Hal Roach
Babes In Toyland – 1934 – Hal Roach
Bonnie Scotland – 1935 – Hal Roach
The Bohemian Girl – 1936 – Hal Roach
Our Relations – 1936 – Hal Roach
Way Out West – 1937 – Hal Roach
Swiss Miss – 1938 – Hal Roach
Blockheads – 1938 – Hal Roach
Flying Deuces – 1939 – Boris Morros
A Chump At Oxford – 1940 – Hal Roach
Saps At Sea – 1940 – Hal Roach
Great Guns – 1941 – Fox
A Haunting We Will Go – 1942 – Fox
Air Raid Wardens – 1943 – MGM
Jitterbugs – 1943 – Fox
Dancing Masters – 1943 – Fox
The Big Noise – 1944 – Fox
The Bullfighters – 1945 – Fox
Nothing But Trouble – 1945 – MGM
Atoll K – 1951 – Fortezza Productions

Six Other Films In Which Laurel and Hardy Appear Together

Lucky Dog – 1917 – Metro
Forty Five Minutes From Hollywood – 1926 – Roach
Hollywood Review of 1929 – MGM
Rogue Song – 1930 – MGM
Hollywood Party of 1934 – MGM
Pick A Star – 1937 – MGM

Finally there are four other little known Laurel and Hardy "guest shots" in various films. Three of them shorts produced by Hal Roach. They are, *On The Loose*, which starred Thelma Todd and ZaSu Pitts, *Wild Poses*, an Our Gang comedy, and *On The Wrong Trek*, starring Charlie Chase. They also made an appearance in the 1931 all-star production of *The Stolen Fools*.

The Marx Brothers

More has been written about the Marx Brothers than any other comedy team in the history of all things funny. For that matter, it might be fair to say that almost more has been written about them than about any single performer in films. There are biographies and autobiographies, memoires and rememberances. And then there is a whole slew of books that "studies" them, dissects their comedy and philosophises on the reasons for their long-lasting success. Sorting through those tomes, putting all the theories into a large vat then boiling them down, you wind up with a list of basics. Call it the Marx Brothers as seen by the sages.

Firstly, say the sages, the Marx Brothers made films that were well constructed. Some better constructed than others. The first five, all done for Paramount, probably the best of the lot. Secondly, say the sages, they had the fortune and insight to work with the best writers of the day . . . George S. Kaufman, S. J. Perelman, Bert Kalmar, Harry Ruby, Arthur Sheekman . . . and then added to those scripts their own natural sense of the lunatic. Thirdly, say the sages, the Marx Brothers were supreme iconoclasts who stopped at nothing to break arms off the deities we hold sacred . . . love, money, politics, sex, education, family, law and order . . . nothing escaped their wrath. Fourthly, say the sages each of their characters was well defined. Zeppo might have been well defined blandness, but then he only made five films before retiring. Chico spoke with an Italian accent. Harpo didn't speak at all. And Groucho spoke every chance he could get.

A list like this might go on forever. *Philosophy Behind Marx Brothers Comedies 101* could probably keep the classrooms full, but lists like this almost always fail to mention the key point. They were popular in their day, and are popular today for one very good and simple reason . . . they were, and they still are, funny!

Born to Sam and Minnie Marx, the boys' early years are certainly as well documented as their film years. Just in case there is anybody on earth who doesn't know, Chico was Leonard and the eldest. Harpo was Adolph, except he eventually changed his name to Arthur. Groucho was Julius, the third son who often said, "I was named after my Uncle Julius who stood well over three feet tall." Milton came next, was called Gummo, but only worked on stage in the beginning and never made any films. Zeppo was last and he too got out of show business early on.

According to Harpo's autobiography, "After Groucho got a taste of the stage, he wanted to be a writer. Chico wanted to be a professional gambler. Gummo wanted to be an inventor. Zeppo wanted to be a prize fighter. I wanted to play the piano on a ferry boat." But Minnie was the classic stage mother. She had helped to make a star of her kid brother Al Schoenberg who went into vaudeville with the name Al Sheen and wound up as half of the famous duo, Gallagher and Sheen. So, she figured, if it worked for her brother, it would work for her sons. She pushed the boys on stage, fought to get them bookings, refused to lose heart when the false starts began to add up, toured with them, and eventually forged a working comedy team out of the oldest three with occasional help from one of the others.

It was in Chicago in 1914 where everything began to come together. Minnie had been *shlepping* her boys around the country to mediocre reviews. In the Windy City, with the reviews getting worse, she rang for Uncle Al who sat down and wrote a comedy routine for the brothers. The act was called *Home Again* featuring Julius as the fast-talking city slicker. He got the laughs. When Leonard and Adolph saw the script, they balked. Adolph didn't have more than a couple of lines and insisted that the situation be changed. So Uncle Al changed it . . . and took out the lines. He convinced Adolph that there was a great tradition in silent clowning, and that was the last time Adolph spoke on stage. Uncle Al then pointed out to Leonard that anyone with an ability to do accents could always get laughs. Leonard immediately became an Italian. He also added his piano playing into the sketch. Adolph now got jealous of Leonard, bought a harp, learned how to play it, and worked that into the act. Milton and Herbert merely faded into the background.

It was while doing *Home Again* that a fellow vaude-villian came up with nicknames for Minnie's boys. Leonard chased girls, known in those days as chickens, so he became Chicko, later Chico. Julius was a constant complainer, hence Groucho. Adolph and his harp made him a natural for Harpo. And Milton's love for gumshoes, if you can believe that, brought him Gummo. When World War I broke out, Gummo was the only one to serve, which brought Herbert into the act. He wound up being called Zeppo, possibly because he was born at the time when the Zeppelins started to arrive in the United States. It's as good a theory as any. After the war, Gummo officially dropped out and Zeppo stayed in.

Home Again was a success in the mid-west and brought them to Broadway, where they had three hits in a row. First was *I'll Say She Is*, then *The Cocoanuts* and finally *Animal Crackers*. While the '20s were still roaring, the Marx Brothers were big stage stars.

And it was on Broadway that they teamed up for the first time with one of the all-time great straight ladies of comedy, Margaret Dumont.

Born around 1890, she was originally a singer whose claim to fame was that she had toured with George M. Cohan in Europe. She was cast in *The Cocoanuts* because the producers felt they needed an actress of dignity and poise to lend legitimate dramatic balance to the particular zaniness of the Marx Brothers. It turned out to be an experience she hadn't quite bargained for. "After three weeks as Groucho's leading lady," she once told an interviewer, "I nearly had a nervous breakdown. He pushed me about, pulled chairs from under me, broiled steaks in the fireplace of my apartment, put frogs in my bath, and made my life miserable on the stage and off. But I don't regret a minute of it. I just love those boys."

The Four Nightingales c.1909 – Groucho, Harpo, Gummo & Lou Levy

The feelings were mutual. "She was a wonderful woman," Groucho explained in his Playboy interview. "She was the same off stage as she was on it, always the stuffy, dignified matron. And the funny thing about her was that she never understood the jokes. Seriously, she never knew what was going on. At the end of *Duck Soup*, we're alone in a small cottage and there's a war going on outside and Margaret says to me, 'What are you doing Rufus?' And I say, 'I'm fighting for your honour, which is more than you ever did.' Later she asked me what I meant by that."

She and Groucho worked so well together that you might say the Marx Brothers were really two distinct comedy teams. Chico and Harpo had their routines. Groucho and Margaret had theirs. His one-liners were funniest when they were bouncing off her. "Martha dear," he says to her in *The Big Store*, "there are many bonds that will hold us together through eternity." She wonders, "Really Wolf? What are they?" He says, "Your government bonds, your savings bonds, your Liberty bonds, and maybe in a year or two after we're married . . ." She cuts in with an anxious, "Yes?" He says, "Who knows, there may be a little baby bond." Now she flutters, "Oh, it all seems so wonderful. Tell me, Wolfie dear, will we have a beautiful home?" Figuring to live off her money, he says, "Of course. You're not planning on moving, are you?" She says, "No, but I'm afraid after we're married a while, a beautiful young girl will come along and you'll forget all about me." Not one to risk hurting her feelings, he assures her, "Don't be silly. I'll write you twice a week."

It was the same kind of thing throughout all the films they did together, like one of the lesser known movies called *At The Circus*. "Get out of this room," she shouts, fending off his amorous advances. "Or I'll scream for the servants." He grabs for her again. "Let the servants know. Let the whole world know."

In some films he's so cruel with her that only her enormous talent for playing straight saves the scene and makes it funny. In *Duck Soup* he swears his love and asks her to marry him. She wonders, "Why, marry you?" He says, "You take me, and I'll take a vacation. I'll need a vacation if we're going to get married. Married. I can see you right now in the kitchen, bending over a hot stove, and I can't see the stove." Also in *Duck Soup*, during a romantic interlude, she asks what he's thinking about. He explains, "Of all the years I wasted collecting stamps. Oh, ah, I suppose you'll think me a sentimental old fluff, but would you mind giving me a lock of your hair." She answers, "A lock of my hair? Why, I had no idea." And he says, "I'm letting you off easy. I was going to ask for the whole wig."

Because Margaret Dumont was physically larger than Groucho, there are entire sets of gags in their films based on their size differences. Not surprisingly, they are always at Margaret Dumont's expense. After she goes through a long speech in one film, for example, he says, "Well, that covers a lot of ground. Say, you cover a lot of ground yourself. You better beat it. I hear they're going to tear you down and put up an office

building where you're standing. You can leave in a taxi. If you can't get a taxi you can leave in a huff. If that's too soon you can leave in a minute and a huff." In another scene together, when she informs him that her husband is dead, he mutters, "I'll bet he's just using that as an excuse." She says, "I was with him till the very end." He says, "No wonder he passed away." She says, "I held him in my arms and kissed him." He says, "Oh I see. Then it was murder."

Margaret Dumont died in 1965, with a long list of films to her credit, among them . . . besides her appearances with the Marx Brothers . . . a role in *Never Give A Sucker An Even Break* with W. C. Fields. But

(Above) Zeppo, Chico, Groucho, Harpo and (far right) Margaret Dumont in the brothers' first film Cocoanuts (1929)

(Overleaf) Chico and Harpo in Horse Feathers (1932)

but they were the first of the great film comics to actually look funny. Chaplin dressed for pathos and owned the most famous walk in films. Groucho dressed for comedy, greasepaint moustache and all, and owned the second most famous walk in films. Laurel and Hardy dressed to show a certain false sense of dignity and played off the differences between fat and thin. Chico and Harpo dressed ridiculously . . . one with an Italian mountaineering hat, the other with a wig, silly hat, baggy pants and a coat as well stocked as any General Store . . . and played off the fact that their ridiculousness was somehow believable . . . that there was a certain sense of logic to it. You might say then that they each dressed to complement their act. Groucho's was the part of the wise-cracking slicker. He had a natural wit, a fast sense of comedy and a terrific team of writers. But no one could really accuse Groucho of ever being a great clown. That role was left to Harpo. Chico, on the other hand, had a very unique job to do in their films, that of a pivot. He was the comic when he worked with Groucho as straightman, and he was the straightman when he worked with Harpo as comic. Still funny more than half a century later, the Chico/Harpo routines seemed to have been based on something that might be called "logical misunderstanding." How wonderful the two of them are when for example, Harpo is trying to explain something to Chico who tries to guess what it is, mixing his Italian accent up with the objects Harpo pulls out of his coat.

Of course of the three, Harpo is probably the only one who could do his act alone. As a mime he's splendid. The way he hands someone his leg to hold. The horn he honks. The way he stands in front of the letters WO leaving only the letters MEN to show until some man walks into the women's restroom and Harpo walks away with glee. Asked for his passport in *Monkey Business*, he pulls a pasteboard from his coat. When told someday he'll have to stop burning his candles at both ends, he reaches into his coat and brings out a candle that is doing just that. When he goes to use a pay phone, he approaches it like a slot machine, puts in his coin, dials his number and wins . . . the phone spits out coins. When told by a cop not to lean against a building, he manages silently to convince the cop that he's leaning there to hold up the building. The cop drags him away and the building falls down. In *Horse Feathers*, when a cop writes out a traffic summons for him, Harpo writes out one for the cop. The cop rips up Harpo's note and so Harpo rips up the cop's note. The cop shows Harpo his badge. Harpo opens his coat to show the cop two dozen badges just like it. The cop motions to Harpo with his nightstick. Harpo grabs the end of it and shakes hands with it. The cop pulls it back. Harpo wraps his hand around it, just above the cop's hand, and suddenly the two of them are going hand over hand up to the top of the stick.

Put a thermometer in Harpo's mouth, and he chews it. Push his stomach and a balloon pops out of his mouth. Chico gets it wrong, Harpo gets it wronger! And yet somehow they manage in the end to get it right. Thoroughly ridiculous, all of it, but throughout it

even if she's terrific with Fields, it still doesn't come close to the work she did with Minnie's boys. She starred with them in seven films, which is interesting because Zeppo only made five films. She really should have been billed as the fourth Marx Brother.

So they hooked up with Margaret Dumont on stage in New York, and took her along with them into the movies. Their first two films were recreations of their stage hits . . . *The Cocoanuts* and *Animal Crackers* . . . and made on Long Island. Then they headed for Hollywood, and comedy material written as films exclusively for them. Not only were they the first legitimate comedy team to go from stage stardom to film stardom,

there's Harpo with a smile on his face and a glint in his eye as if to hint that he's laughing too.

Long after the brothers made their final film together, Chico and Harpo proved that the two of them had been a team all along, and a great one at that. They worked together in a short made for television which sadly doesn't seem to get re-run very often. It's called *The Great Jewel Robbery*, and even though critics panned it, the film is good fun. It's almost completely silent . . the only spoken line comes from a surprise appearance by Groucho at the very end. As part of the General Electric Theatre on the American network

CBS in 1959, Chico and Harpo go about stealing all sorts of odd things, such as salamis, which they then use in an elaborate heist of a jeweller's shop. The salami serves to help paint a stolen car to look like a police car in black and white. Harpo then dresses like Groucho, goes into a jeweller's and holds it up. Chico, dressed like a cop, comes in to arrest Harpo. Thinking they've gotten away with it, they try to make their getaway only to discover that their black and white police car is the exact opposite of the city's white and black police cars. The last scene, during the police line-up, is when Groucho appears to announce, "We won't say a word

48

(Above) Herbert, Arthur, Leonard & Julius Marx

(Right) The poster advertising the Marx Brothers' first film, Cocoanuts

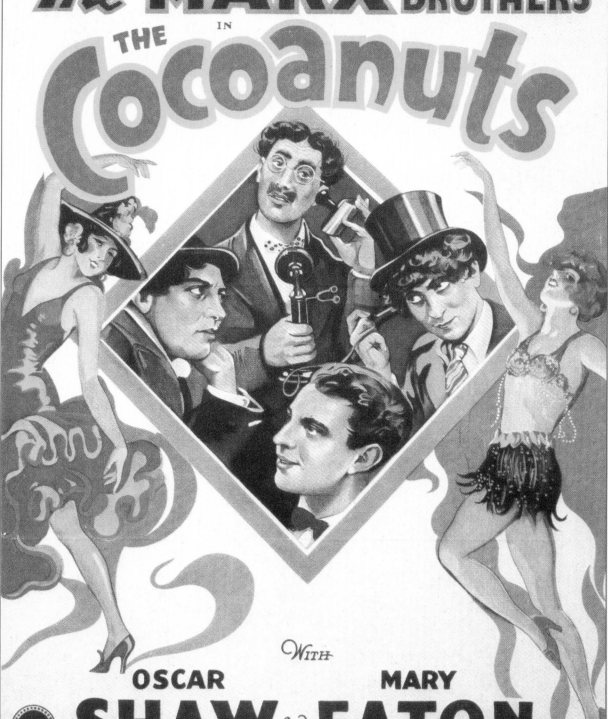

Paramount's
All Talking-Singing
MUSICAL COMEDY *HIT!*
The MARX BROTHERS
IN
THE Cocoanuts

WITH

OSCAR SHAW AND MARY EATON

until we've spoken with our lawyers."

It was never meant to be immortal comedy, but it's a half hour of wonderful silent comedy, and great fun to watch Chico and Harpo working alone.

The Marx Brothers as a group of four, then three, only made thirteen films. *The Cocoanuts* was officially their first, although it seems that somewhere around 1926 there was a film in progress, *Humor Risk*, which the brothers made privately and never finished. Harpo was actually the first of the family to make a film appearance, having had a minor part in the 1925 picture *Too Many Kisses* with William Powell also in the cast.

Once the brothers moved to Hollywood to work for Paramount, they made three more films as a gang of four. And those first five are the ones the purists generally consider to be the best. In 1935, when Zeppo dropped out, the three others moved to MGM where they did eight films over a fourteen year period. *A Night At The Opera* was their first for MGM, and probably the best they did there, thanks to Irving Thalberg, a young producer who had an inborn understanding of what the Marx Brothers were trying to accomplish. A card playing friend of Chico's, Thalberg was one of the young wizards of Hollywood. Given the chance to develop material for the brothers, he insisted their routines be tried before a live audience. He sent the entire cast of *A Night At The Opera* on tour for two months as if they were a vaudeville act. Writers tagged along to punch up the script whenever audiences proved it was necessary. It was a very novel approach to film rehearsal and scriptwriting and it definitely paid off. Probably the best known of any Marx Brothers film routine was the famous stateroom scene from that film. To make the story of the routine even better, it was almost cut. The first few times the brothers went through the sketch on the road, the audiences didn't respond. The hired typewriters called back to Hollywood to tell Thalberg they were taking it out of the show. But then the Marx brothers added their own touch. As Harpo explained it in his autobiography, "As written, a bunch of guys jamming into a stateroom for no good reason, this bit failed to get a laugh on stage. The writers got very depressed over it and decided to cut it. We decided, however, to give it one more chance. So this night we did it our way. Groucho, ordering a meal from a steward while being jostled into the corner of the jammed stateroom said, 'And a hard boiled egg.' I honked my horn. 'Make it two hard boiled eggs,' said Groucho. The audience broke up, and as simply as that, a dud became a classic."

Thalberg was so thrilled that his theory had proved correct, he committed MGM to the expense of sending the cast on the road again for try-outs of their next film effort, *A Day At The Races*. Again the script was polished into a neat bit of vaudeville to be translated to film. But before this picture was in the can, Thalberg suddenly died. He was only in his 30s, making his death all the more shocking. And with hindsight that death might have marked the beginning of the end for the Marx Brothers as a successful working comedy

A Day At The Races *(1937)*

957-65

A 1932 promotional give-away for the Marxes fourth movie, Horse Feathers

The poster design for the Marxes last Paramount movie, Duck Soup

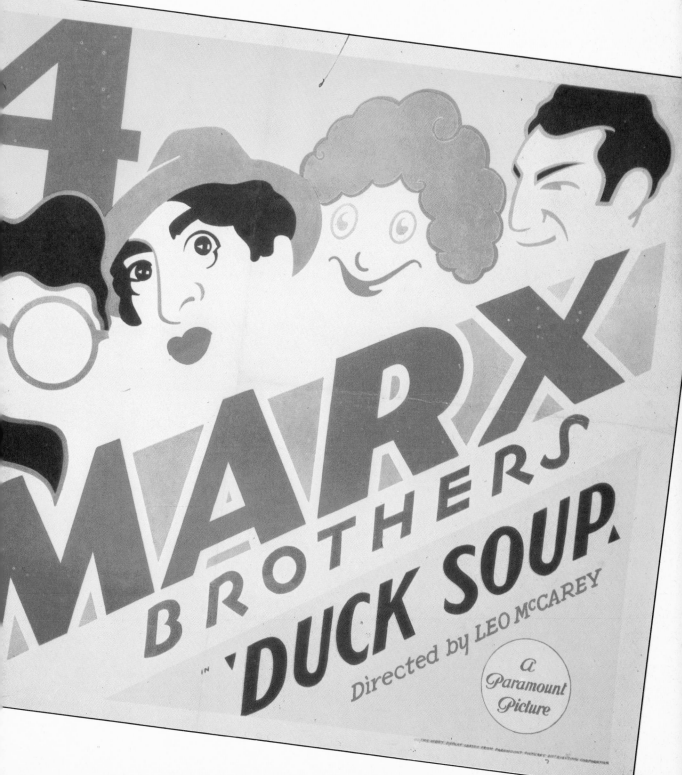

team. They continued to make movies but with the exception of some scenes here and there, the Marx Brothers never really managed to reach the same heights they had once found. In only two films, Thalberg had become an invaluable silent partner.

By the time World War II broke out, the Marx Brothers decided they had gone as far as they could and they officially retired. *The Big Store* was released that year. It was their eleventh film. And it was far from what audiences a decade before had come to expect. Rather than suffer the fate of so many aging comics, they chose to fold up their tents and steal away into radio and television and semi-retirement. But United Artists came along in 1946 with a camp take-off of a Humphrey Bogart/Ingrid Bergman epic, and as a Marx Brothers film, *A Night In Casablanca* isn't all that bad. However, in the book of his collected ramblings to friends, Groucho immortalises *A Night In Casablanca* through a series of letters to the Warner Brothers legal department who tried to stop the film from happening. As reprinted in *The Groucho Letters*, it seems the Warner Brothers threatened legal action against the Marx Brothers if they insisted on sending up the Bogart/Bergman classic. Groucho penned a long letter

to the Brothers Warner, including the comment, "You claim you own *Casablanca* and that no one else can use that name without your permission. What about 'Warner Brothers'? Do you own that too? You probably have the right to use the name Warner, but what about Brothers? Professionally we were brothers long before you were."

The Warners' legal department responded, asking for a brief outline of *A Night In Casablanca*, which Groucho provided . . . although his version of the story didn't exactly resemble the film as we know it. He wrote, "There are many scenes of splendour and fierce antagonisms, and Colour, an Abyssinian messenger boy runs Riot. Riot, in case you have never been there, is a small night club on the edge of town."

When the Warners' lawyers wrote back that they didn't understand a thing about the plot of the film, Groucho wrote yet another letter saying that he had just received a new version of the plot, and explained, "In the fifth reel, Gladstone makes a speech that sets the House of Commons in an uproar and the King promptly asks for his resignation. Harpo marries a hotel detective. Chico operates an ostrich farm. Humphrey Bogart's girl Bordello spends her last years in a Bacall house."

It was the last Groucho heard from the Warners.

One of the faintly amusing things about seeing all thirteen of their films again is spotting faces in the crowd. Some strange people showed up in Marx Brothers pictures. Maureen O'Sullivan, for example, is in *A Day At The Races*. Lucille Ball appears in *Room Service*. Eve Arden is in *At The Circus*. Tony Martin is in *The Big Store*. And in *Love Happy*, the last of the Marx Brothers films, there's not only Raymond Burr . . . later to be Perry Mason and Ironside . . . but also a very young Marilyn Monroe.

Once they split up as a film comedy team, each of the three brothers continued working in various ways. Groucho was, however, far more successful as a single act than either Chico or Harpo. He made guest appear-

ances in several films, including *Mr. Music* with Bing Crosby in 1950, and with Frank Sinatra and Jane Russell in the 1951 picture *Double Dynamite*. He also appeared in *A Girl In Every Port*, *Will Success Spoil Rock Hunter?* and Otto Preminger's film *Skidoo*. In 1957 the three brothers showed up in *The Story Of Mankind*, each working alone. Groucho played Peter Minuit, buying Manhatten Island from the Indians. Chico was cast as a monk in another scene. And Harpo played Isaac Newton. Of course, on television, Groucho's dramatic triumph might have come when he starred in a production of *The Mikado*, although he is never to be forgotten for his wise-cracking in the long running and now often rerun camp TV quiz show, *You Bet Your Life*.

Harpo, Zeppo, Chico, Groucho and Gummo

The Films of The Marx Brothers

With Groucho, Chico, Harpo and Zeppo

(Humor Risk – 1925 – privately produced by the brothers and never completed.)

The Cocoanuts – 1929 – Paramount
Animal Crackers – 1930 – Paramount
Monkey Business – 1931 – Paramount
Horse Feathers – 1932 – Paramount
Duck Soup – 1933 – Paramount

With only Groucho, Chico and Harpo

A Night At The Opera – 1935 – MGM
A Day At The Races – 1937 – MGM
Room Service – 1938 – RKO
At The Cricus – 1939 – MGM
Go West – 1940 – MGM
The Big Store – 1941 – MGM
A Night In Casablanca – 1946 – United Artists
Love Happy – 1949 – United Artists

A contemporary ad. for Why Bring That Up?

The Ritz Brothers

In the beginning there was Coney Island, Jimmy Durante, a brother named George and a sister named Gertrude.

George became their manager, Gertrude went off to live her own life, Jimmy Durante got better bookings and Coney Island became proof positive of Gresham's Law. As for the Ritz Brothers, they went on to become filmdom's most unique comedy team . . . unique in the sense that either you understood them and thought they were the best invention since canned beer, or you stared blankly at the big screen and wondered what the hell was going on. Unlike all the other teams, with the Ritz Brothers, there was nothing in between.

The way one critic so aptly put it, "The movies never knew what to do with the Ritz Brothers, and in return, the Ritz Brothers never quite knew what to do with the movies." Yet the people who thought they were funny are almost unfaltering in their opinion that no group . . . not even the Marxes . . . have ever been funnier.

That's what got them to Coney Island in the first place.

Come to think of it, that's what got them out of there too.

All three were born in Newark, New Jersey during the opening decade of the 20th century. Al was first in 1903. Then came Jimmy in 1905. Finally there was Harry in 1908. The family name was Joachim . . . their parents were immigrants from Austria . . . and the three boys, with brother George and sister Gertrude grew up in Brooklyn where they all attended PS 147. During those years Al Joachim fancied himself as a pretty good dancer and found that when he entered local dance contests he could sometimes win. When school got in the way of his dance contests, school was left behind. Al and his best friend . . . a Brooklyn kid named George Raft who would also eventually make his way to Hollywood . . . decided to take their dancing contests career one-step further, and they found themselves in vaudeville. They were, as the expression went, hoofers.

Somewhere around the beginning of the 1920s, Jimmy and Harry also showed an interest in vaudeville. But it wasn't until 1925 that brother George managed to convince Al, Jimmy and Harry to join forces as a team. The three agreed and George found a role for himself as their agent. He got them into the office of a booking agent who said he could probably get them work, but that they'd have to change their name. It seems that having a handle like "The Joachim Brothers" wasn't on. Not knowing what to do . . . at least this is the way the story goes . . . one of the brothers looked out the window and saw a passing truck. It happened to have been from the Ritz Laundry.

Their professional debut came at a Coney Island dive in 1925, on a bill with Jimmy Durante. Their success on the boardwalk got them booked "uptown" . . . at Fox's Folly Theatre in Brooklyn. Their act was described as "lowbrow zaniness", and the crowds loved it. Suddenly the Ritz Brothers were vaudevillians.

Stardom, however, didn't exactly come overnight.

Like the Marxes, they toured and worked and learned their trade, playing such high spots as opening act to an exotic dancer named Gilda Gray. But it was while working with Gilda that they were spotted by Earl Carroll who immediately signed them up for his *Vanities Of 1932*. Interestingly enough, the three brothers might have seemed vaguely familiar to Carroll. They had worked for him once before, briefly, in a show called *The Florida Girl* where they were billed as Al Socrates, Jimmy Plato and Harry Aristotle.

From *Vanities Of 1932*, they worked their way up to *Continental Vanities* which opened in late 1934. Their act was one of mayhem . . . it was fashionable for brothers in those days . . . but these three didn't necessarily rely on funny costumes or such well defined characterisations as certain other brothers. The Ritzes based their act on funny mayhem. The kind that appealed to someone at a small firm known as Educational Pictures, who hired them for a two-reeler, *Hotel Anchovy*. During the eighteen minutes that the film runs, the three brothers as employees of the hotel wreak absolute mayhem. And when this short appeared in the 1963 film *The Sound Of Laughter*, it was still very funny.

Within a couple of years the three were not only top-billed vaudeville comics but also just what Darryl Zanuck figured he needed to back up some musicals 20th Century Fox was going to produce. The brothers were working a club in Los Angeles at the time, Zanuck had seen *Hotel Anchovy*, and signing them seemed like the logical thing to do. Their first feature film was *Sing Baby Sing*, starring Alice Faye and Adolph Menjou.

Loosely based on a popular romance of the day between Elaine Barrie and John Barrymore, the storyline is something about a cabaret singer and a Shakespearean actor who save each other's career. The Ritz Brothers play a burlesque comedy team, and for the most part have nothing at all to do with the plot. Like almost all the other comedy teams who start making movies, the first film is just an excuse to let them do their routine on film. They clown and raise mayhem, and even sing *The Music Goes Round* as if it were an opera. When the film ends and the credits have rolled, the Ritz Brothers actually make a celluloid curtain call. In an obvious attempt to tell the country just who these three are, Zanuck let them have a bow after the film was over. It's one of those strange things that might never have been done before, and certainly hasn't been done very often since. But it made the point. The critics remembered their name and gave them credit for bringing, "A new type of crazy fooling to the screen."

Immediately Zanuck signed them to a longer term contract and tossed them into four films in 1937. In the first three they were the "specialty act" . . . the comics who sang and danced and generally clowned around without getting in the way of the plot. In *One In A Million*, starring Sonja Henie, the Ritz Brothers steal the show on ice-skates, doing their imitation of Boris Karloff, Charles Laughton and Peter Lorre. In *On The Avenue*, starring Dick Powell and Alice Faye, Harry Ritz does his drag act for the first time, and the brothers

(This page) Hope & Crosby *in* Road To Bali

(Right) Dean Martin and Jerry Lewis in The Stooge *(1953)*

(l to r) Jimmy, Harry and Al in You Can't Have Everything *(1937)*

sing *Slumming On Park Avenue*. In *You Can't Have Everything* they made their third appearance with Alice Faye and do an absolutely hilarious number called *Long Underwear*. So successful were those three efforts, that for their fourth venture of 1937, they were given starring roles. The film was *Life Begins In College* . . . the British title was *The Joy Parade* . . . and while the Ritz's usual brand of mayhem is funny in itself, the film was a fairly tired one.

Not letting that worry him, Samuel Goldwyn liked what he saw of the Ritz Brothers and rented them from Darryl Zanuck for his production of *The Goldwyn Follies*, which was nothing more than a fancy vaudeville revue. The Ritz Brothers performed their *Serenade To A Fish* number dressed as mermaids, and

were probably the only good things about the film.

Returning to 20th Century Fox, the Ritz Brothers then found themselves in a strange situation. Everyone knew that they were funny but in the film business you're only as good as your last film, and their last two were not so hot. Zanuck agreed they were stars, but now he only sent them B comedies. B perhaps in terms of budget and the talent he added to the costs. And B perhaps in the eyes of the critics who might have chuckled here and there. But all these years later they really should be considered classic Ritz Brothers.

The first was called *Kentucky Moonshine* in the States and *Three Men And A Girl* in England.

A famous radio producer is looking for some hillbillies for one of his programmes. Because they want to

do their act on the programme, the Ritz Brothers with Marjorie Weave in tow, head from New York to Kentucky where they impersonate hillbillies. While there, they're mistaken for the real thing by a neighbouring clan and wind up in the middle of a long-standing family feud. Impressed with what he's found, the famous radio producer decides to use them . . until he finds out that they're not the genuine article. Confusion reigns and the three cavort about to such an extent that if anyone, up to this point, ever mistook the Ritzes for just a rip-off of the Marxes, they certainly didn't think that way for long.

"Unlike those sturdy individualists the Marx Brothers," wrote one reviewer, "the Ritzes work as a team but their clowning is varied and vigorous enough to avoid the impression that they are producing a series of photographed vaudeville turns. The story is more of a setting for them. It gathers force and pace from their crazy antics."

Starring with them was singer Tony Martin and none other than the wonderful character actor, Slim Summerville. It might have been one of his best films as well.

The second of the two B-comedies dated 1938 was *Straight, Place and Show*, with the British title being *They're Off*. Ethel Merman worked as the brothers' leading lady. But at this point the Ritz Brothers must have seen their career getting locked forever into such films. The only way out, they decided, was to make a stand. So they went to Zanuck and said they wanted better films to do, or else. It was a brave move because most of the moguls running Hollywood in those days could have cared less about the "or else," and simply shown them to the door. They didn't get where they were by backing down to vain threats yet, this time, Zanuck did back down. No one really knows why . . . except possibly because he too believed in their ability to get big laughs.

He sent them comedic immortality in the form of their next film, *The Three Musketeers*. It is not only one of their all-time funniest films, it might also be one of the best versions ever done of the Dumas story. The script stayed relatively faithful to the original, the cast was peppered with big names such as Don Ameche, and the Ritzes were terrific. If they ever had a secret to their comedy it might have been their timing and in this film it was never better. An especially funny touch to the script was that the brothers didn't actually play the Musketeers themselves. Through a rather large slice of licence with the Dumas story, the real Musketeers are waylaid and the Ritz Brothers become imposters.

Today the picture is considered a Ritz Brothers classic. In 1939 it was funny and well accepted by the public, but the critics only came up with mixed reviews. "The Three Musketeers is too Ritz a mixture for our taste," punned the New York Times, perhaps a bit weary of the brothers usual mayhem.

That might have been the reaon why Darryl Zanuck sent along their next script from the B-comedy file. It was called *The Gorilla* and when the Ritz Brothers read it, they said no. This time, however, Zanuck didn't

back down. The brothers walked out. Zanuck threatened to sue. And only then did the brothers come back. They made the picture begrudgingly. Their opinion of the film was quite correct. It was followed by *Pack Up Your Troubles* . . . the British title was *We're In The Army Now* . . . and once that was in the can the Brothers Ritz packed up their trunks and moved off the Zanuck lot. They felt they deserved better, and knew they were still big enough names in vaudeville that they could continue working until a good film came along.

They didn't have all that long to wait, but then what came along wasn't another *Three Musketeers*. It was *Argentine Nights*.

Universal Studios put them in a musical that was the screen debut of the Andrews Sisters. The Ritzes had very little to do with the plot of the film. They did a few of their standard routines, such as all three of them eating a hero sandwich at the same time, and they also did their imitation of the Andrews Sisters singing a number. But no matter how much they clowned, something was missing. No matter what they did, something was wrong.

Looking back it's easy to see what was happening. The studios weren't getting enough feedback from films like *The Gorilla* to warrant a big investment in new material for the Ritzes, which meant they had to rely on material that was tried and tested, and, unfortunately, a bit tired. That meant the critics were beginning to yawn which also meant that the studios were faced with the consequences of their own actions. At Universal, for instance, money was being spent on Abbott and Costello. So the management shrugged. What did they need with a comedy team who couldn't keep up?

The Ritz Brothers went back to vaudeville.

But in 1942 they called the Ritz Brothers again and offered them a three picture contract. Who knows why? Maybe the bosses at Universal felt that all the Ritzes needed was great material. If that was the case, then why were the three films offered the brothers among the weakest of their career? Who knows how Hollywood thinks!

The three films were *Behind The Eight Ball* . . . in England it was called *Off The Beaten Track* . . . followed by *Hiya Chum* . . . the British title of this one was *Everything Happens To Us* . . . and then *Never A Dull Moment*. None of them can be considered classic comedies, but there are bits and pieces in each of them where the Ritz Brothers truly shine. *Behind The Eight Ball* is best described as a comedy-thriller, complete with a murder weapon that turns out to be hidden in a clarinet. At times the film borders on silliness, yet one critic wrote about it then, "The plot matters far less than the turns. The Ritz Brothers are unceasingly funny and there is plenty of music and song so that the murders are incidental only."

The plot didn't matter much at all in *Hiya Chum*, a picture which should have been called *The Road To Hollywood*. The critics called it a yawn. It has something to do with three vaudevillians and two girls who head for stardom in Los Angeles but wind up stranded

(This page) The Three Musketeers *(1939)*

(Right) In Argentine Nights *with the Andrews Sisters (1940)*

in the boondocks where they are suddenly stuck in the middle of some shady goings-on. There is singing and clowning . . . and the bits and pieces of brilliance are fewer and farther between.

As for *Never A Dull Moment*, who said so? It was a most unfortunate title for the final Ritz Brother picture. Called "A Crook Musical" in one studio press release, the brothers get involved with the theft of a diamond necklace at a party. They should have stayed home. It's really too bad because given the kind of material that some other comics of the era were getting, they could have finished their movie career as the funniest men in America. As it was, they saw the rushes, realised that their California days were over and headed back to the stage. Worthy of their talent, they were the first real star comedy act to play Las Vegas. Now the Mecca of saloon comics, the Ritz Brothers opened the town, appearing at El Rancho, then the only club on the famous strip. Years later they played such places as The Flamingo, The Dunes and The Sands. During the '50s there was some television, although strangely enough they never got a series the way so many other comedy teams did . . . the way Abbott and Costello did . . . and finally in 1965, while the three were playing a club in New Orleans, Al died of a heart attack.

Troupers that they were, Harry and Jimmy decided to carry on. They restyled their nightclub routine for a duo, and worked wherever they could. In 1975 they appeared with Robert Livingston and Yvonne de Carlo in *Blazing Stewardesses*, where they performed a bunch of their old gags. They also worked as a duo for exactly one minute in *Won Ton Ton—The Dog Who Saved Hollywood*. And while neither of those films could possibly be mistaken for anything like memorable cinema, each of them had enough of the Ritz touch prove the brothers still had what it takes.

66

In 1976, Harry worked alone in a film. Appropriately it was Mel Brooks' *Silent Movie*. And the reason it was so fitting is because Brooks himself used a few Ritz Brothers routines in that film. When Brooks and Dom De Luise and Marty Feldman dance together, it is pure Ritz Brothers.

Maybe someday the world will rediscover them. Ask any professional comedian about them and chances are he'll say that they were great, that they should be rated somewhere near the top. Their entry in one of those endless encyclopedias about people who have passed through Hollywood unfairly makes a kind of comparison with the Marx Brothers. "They lacked the anarchic abandon of the comic brilliance of the Marx Brothers," Ephraim Katz wrote, "but in their own way proved a successful team and for a while were quite popular with the public, if not most critics.'

Maybe what someone should say is that they were a comedy team worthy of being called comedians' comics.

The Films of the Ritz Brothers

Hotel Anchovy – 1934 – Educational
Sing Baby, Sing – 1936 – 20th Century-Fox
One In A Million – 1937 – 20th Century-Fox
On The Avenue – 1937 – 20th Century-Fox
You Can't Have Everything – 1937 – 20th Century-Fox
Life Begins In College – 1937 – 20th Century-Fox
The Goldwyn Follies – 1938 – United Artists
Kentucky Moonshine – 1938 – 20th Century-Fox
Straight, Place and Show – 1938 – 20th Century-Fox
The Three Musketeers – 1939 – 20th Century-Fox
The Gorilla – 1939 – 20th Century-Fox
Pack Up Your Troubles – 1939 – 20th Century-Fox
Argentine Nights – 1940 – Universal
Behind The Eight Ball – 1943 – Universal
Hiya Chum – 1943 – Universal
Never A Dull Moment – 1943 – Universal

Hope, Crosby + Lamour

They weren't really meant to be part of a series. At least not in the beginning. The "Road" pictures were done one by one. And it took more than two decades to do all seven. Yet now, more than twenty years since the last "Road" flick was put into the can, Bob Hope, Bing Crosby and Dorothy Lamour are unmistakably as much a comedy team in their own right as the "Road" pictures are a series.

Seven films, held together by three familiar faces, made funny by carefully mixing throw away lines with visual comedy to recreate a certain charm once found on radio. And without radio, the "Road" pictures probably would never have happened.

As the 1930s started drawing to a close, radio was firmly established in America as the family's first line of entertainment. Vaudeville, the stage show, was suffering. For the most part, burlesque was gone. The stars had abandoned the six-shows-a-day grind for the easy work/big money areas of film and radio. And sure, Hollywood was at the height of what might be called the movies' greatest era. But, in order to take in a film you had to leave the house. Listening to radio was something you could do with your slippers on in the comfort of your own living-room. There were weekly visits from "The Shadow" who knew what evils lay in

the hearts of men, and who spent thirty minutes one night a week bringing those evils to justice. Then there was Bing to "croon" his latest single. And a whole slew of folk to make the country laugh. Fields. Benny. Burns and Allen. Bob Hope. Fred Allen. Amos 'n' Andy. Fibber McGee and Molly. But when it came to comedy, radio had the same effect on material that television continues to have today . . . all consuming. With ten or fifteen million people tuning in to your jokes, you could only use them once. In the beginning of radio, vaudeville routines worked as well as they did when vaudeville first went to the movie lots. But they wore out quickly. Radio comedy eased into a more intimate style, a low-key approach that gave radio a "folksy", more "livingroom and slippers" feel.

By the time radio comedies were heading west to debut in the movies, it was movie comedy that changed. Films took on that radio flavour. And the "Road" pictures were born.

Starting with Bing and Bob doing their radio patter, Hollywood developed a formula that worked in all seven of the "Road" films. One element is a romantic setting. Another is the plot . . . it should include some friendly competition for the heroine's love, five or six songs, and enough asides to the camera to make it seem

Bob Hope and Bing Crosby in the first 'Road' movie – Road To
Singapore *(1940)*

as if Hope and Crosby were actually making fun of the film. Whether they were fortune hunting or trying to make their own fortune by selling a better mousetrap, they must always come off looking like good-hearted con men. Dorothy Lamour can be the object of everyone's affections but, because Bing is the straightman, he wins the girl. He can be the conniver, but Bob must then be the innocent victim. If Bob gets into trouble . . . funny trouble . . . he must somehow try to drag Bing into it with him.

Hope isn't Chaplin. Crosby isn't Barrymore. And Lamour isn't Jane Fonda. But they clicked and that was enough to make the "Road" pictures work.

Of course, each of them was already a star when they made the first one, *The Road To Singapore*.

Bing was born with the name of Harry Lillis Crosby, and had been a band singer with Paul Whiteman before going into films with Mack Sennett in 1931. From there he went into radio and, by the time he returned to films, he was the first successful radio singer to become established as a film star.

Bob was born Leslie Towne Hope, and had been a vaudevillian before going into radio, then films. Whilst he could sing a little, and do a competent soft-shoe, he built his reputation on his ability to wise-crack. He could always come up with the right line which, at the same time as being funny, also had a somewhat self-effacing quality to it. "Bing's my oldest friend," he would say. "We often play golf together, you know. But that's all over. Would you play golf with a guy who cheats? A guy who picks up the ball when nobody's looking and throws it towards the hole? Of course you wouldn't. Neither will Crosby."

Dorothy Lamour was born Mary Leta Dorothy Kaumeyer and was voted Miss New Orleans in 1931. She worked as a band singer in Chicago, before becoming a radio performer, and then going on to wear a sarong in a film which so scandalized middle-America that she became a star.

Lamour and Hope worked together in Bob's first film, *The Big Broadcast Of 1938*, a Paramount effort. It was a film worth noting because in it Bob Hope sang *Thanks For The Memory*. Trivia fans will be delighted to know that he sang it with Shirley Ross. The song won an Academy Award and immediately became Hope's theme song. Bob and Bing made their screen debut together in a little known film later that same year. It was a short that Paramount put together about golf called *Don't Hook Now*. But it wasn't until 1940 that Bob, Bing and Dorothy became the inseperable team that wound their way through seven pictures "on the road."

The script for *The Road To Singapore* had been sitting on various desks at Paramount for quite a while. The studio executives wanted to make the film but they weren't sure who to cast. For a while there was talk about using Fred MacMurray and Jack Oakie. Also on the list of possibles was George Burns and Gracie Allen. You can only guess what might have happened to any of their careers had they won the roles. As it turned out, the names Hope, Crosby and Lamour finally emerged

With Judith Barrett in Road To Singapore

(Overleaf) Road To Zanzibar *(1941)*

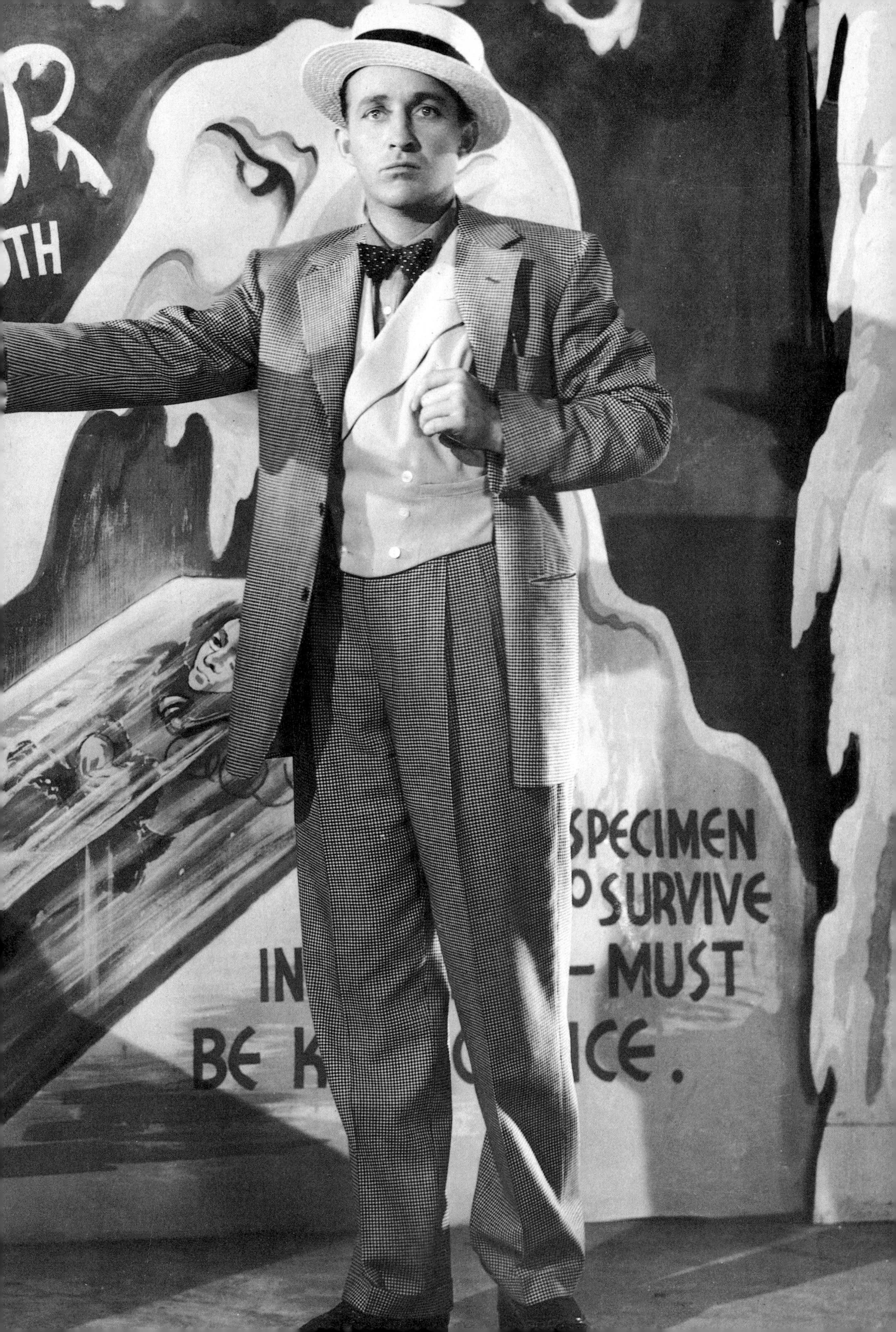
TH
SPECIMEN
SURVIVE
IN — MUST
BE K ICE.

on top, and the picture swung into production.

Written by two talented and funny guys, Frank Butler and Don Hartman . . . the same pair who would also do the next two "Road" pictures . . . the supporting cast included Charles Coburn, Anthony Quinn and Jerry Colonna. The storyline is about marriage . . . or rather, how to avoid getting married. Bing plays Josh and Bob plays Ace, two friends just back from sea who are rudely informed that Ace will be forced to marry. A trap had been set to catch him, and once they punch their way out of it, they are then told by Josh's father that Josh has been betrothed and will also have to marry. The answer for both is a fast trip out of town . . . all the way to Kaigoon, an island south of Singapore. That's where Josh and Ace bump into Mima, played by Dorothy Lamour. She is a dancer who needs saving from the evil Caesar, which is just what Josh and Ace manage to do. But when they wake up the next morning, they find that Mima has pawned all of their worldly goods to buy food, and plans on moving in with them. Stuck for funds, Ace decides to sell spot remover to the natives . . . except the spot remover doesn't work, and usually leaves a worse spot than the one it was supposed to remove. It also leaves Josh and Ace and Mima in the awkward situation of having to flee from the dissatisfied customers. They head for the hills where they "go native" by dressing themselves in table cloths and turbans. During a native feast, Ace wonders about a certain dance which seems to be followed by boys and girls going off together into the forest. He's told it's the marriage ceremony, which Josh unknowingly is in the midst of. Trying to save his friend, he's stopped when, out of nowhere, Josh's father shows up with the girl betrothed to Josh. But Josh says he loves Mima. Now so does Ace. They decide to let her choose between them and she chooses Ace, even though she secretly loves Josh. Dejected, Josh leaves on an around the world trip with his father and betrothed. Then the cops show up looking for Ace . . . they don't like the way he's been selling that spot remover . . . and he and Mima are forced to escape. They sail home. During the trip Ace comes to understand that Mima really loves Josh, who just happens to find them when they arrive home. Mima falls into his arms. The cops try to nab Ace . . . and now the three of them run off together.

The whole business was so ridiculous that it struck 1940 audiences as being very funny. The difference between this first "Road" film and all the others is a minor one, in that here it's Hope who does all the scheming. In the others, it's Crosby. The film worked so well, the producers decided to try another one just like it. Butler and Hartman sat down at their typewriters, changed the setting, in some ways simplified the plot, and basically came up with the same movie.

In *The Road To Zanzibar*, Bing is called Chuck and Bob is called Fearless. They're working in a carnival where Fearless happens to be the fairly reluctant human cannon ball. "I don't mind being drafted," he says as Bing stuffs him into the cannon's muzzle, "but not for ammunition." When he's fired, a dummy shoots through the air, slams into a tent, inadvertently causes a fire and the carnival burns to the ground. Chuck and Fearless must escape. Instead of running to Singapore, they head for darkest Africa. There they come across the beautiful slavegirl Donna . . . Dorothy Lamour . . . being sold on the market by a woman named Julia, played un Una Merkel. They buy Donna, not realizing that she and Julia have worked it out to split the profits. Donna then tells them that she must go to see her father who lives on the other side of Africa. Fearless is suspicious but Chuck falls for her story and organizes a safari. It's not until they find themselves deep in the heart of jungle that they discover this is just a story Donna has invented to get transported across the continent so that she can go to the rich man who has promised to marry her.

Annoyed at being used, Chuck and Fearless abandon Donna, leaving her with the native guides, and try to go back on their own. Immediately they fall into the hands of a savage tribe. Their only hope for survival is to wrestle with, and beat, the tribe's highly esteemed ape. Naturally it's Chuck who volunteers Fearless' services to wrestle the gorilla. Naturally they manage to get away, finally arriving back at the coast where they plan to buy tickets for the journey home. But when Chuck takes their money and goes off to purchase the tickets, he comes back with Donna and Julia who were still working their slave girl scam. Now Donna admits she has fallen for Chuck, and the four of them decide they'll all sail back to America. But tickets for four cost twice as much as tickets for two, so Fearless works out a scheme to raise money. They'll do a few magic tricks . . . like sawing a woman in half. And just as they begin their performance, Bing asks, "You sure you know how to do this?" Saw in hand, Bob closes the film with, "if not, one of us will go back half fare."

Besides the similarity in the plots, a number of gags also reappear in the second film. One of them is the "Pat-a-cake" routine. Whenever Bob and Bing have to fight their way out of a situation, instead of immediately throwing punches they play the children's game of pat-a-cake . . . slapping their hands together to a familiar rhyme. They then punch whoever is standing nearby. They used it several times in *Singapore*, and it became a kind of signal to the audience that a fight would happen. At one point in *Zanzibar*, with the villain lurking nearby, they begin the routine, only to be punched first by the villain. Hope's retort, 'He must have seen the picture." That's the first time that either Hope or Crosby step out of a picture with an aside. It's a gag they used throughout the rest of the "Road" pictures, and because they actually make fun of themselves, it might be the most endearing of all the running gags.

It was certainly one of the devices that gave the "Road" films that familiar, relaxed radio programme quality. And because it worked so well in *Zanzibar*, they made sure they used it several times in the next epic, *The Road To Morocco*.

The third of the "Road" pictures in as many years, this one is probably the best of the Butler/Hartman efforts, and looking back, it might well be the best of

the Hope and Crosby and Lamour efforts as well. "Just like Webster's Dictionary," they sang, "we're Morocco bound." Bing played Jeff and Bob played Turkey, and as they ride across the desert on the back of a camel, the aside comes, 'I'll lay you eight to five that we'll meet Dorothy Lamour." That's followed with the assurance that no matter what the adventure is, "Paramount won't let anything happen to us. We're signed for five more years." Later, as Hope starts to explain the plot, Crosby cuts in with, "I know that." Hope says, "Yeah, but the people who came in the middle of the picture don't." Crosby asks astoundedly, "You mean they missed my song?" The asides in this one go so far astray from the main line of the film, that there is even a camel who looks right at the camera and mumbles, "This is the screwiest picture I was ever in."

The Road To Morocco is also the picture that got Hope and Crosby and Lamour started on outlandish sight gags. Bob, wearing curved-toed Arab shoes gets kissed by Dorothy, and the shoes uncurl. "Now kiss him on the nose," suggests Bing, "and see if you can straighten that out."

The plot, which becomes less and less important with each film, gets Jeff and Turkey to Morocco by using the device of having them shipwrecked off the coast. In need of money, Jeff sells Turkey for 2,500 kolacks. But later that night in the middle of a bad dream, he regrets the act and tries to find his friend. Turkey, in the meantime, has been taken to the royal palace where he is to be married by the woman who bought him, Princess Shalmar, played by Dorothy Lamour. Jeff immediately sets out to change places with Turkey. At the same time, the desert chieftain Mullay, played by a fierce Anthony Quinn, hears of the impending marriage, feels jilted and insists on an explanation from the Princess' private counsellor. He tells Mullay not to worry because it is written in the stars that the Princess' first husband will die within a week of the marriage. Turkey learns of his fate when he comes across a pair of guys carving his epitaph in stone. He then suggests Jeff take over as fiancé. All looks good for Jeff . . . at least he thinks so . . . until the private counsellor realizes he made a mistake in his prediction about the marriage, and tries to convince the Princess not to proceed with it and that she must marry Mullay. Shalmar, however, has fallen for Jeff and wants to go ahead with the wedding. Mullay decides to take the matter into his own hands, and kidnaps Jeff and Turkey. Shalmar sends them a magic ring, which Turkey puts on and mumbles, "Well, I'll be a

(Overleaf) With Dorothy Lamour in Road To Rio *(1948)*

monkey's uncle." It transforms him instantly into a monkey. The monkey escapes the cell, defeats the guards, and transforms back into Turkey who helps Jeff escape. The two put on the guards' costumes, darken their faces and try to infiltrate the wedding of Shalmar and Mullay. By sprinkling gun powder into the pipe tobacco, they cause a total riot, during which Jeff and Turkey and Shalmar run off together into the night. Sounds familiar?

As one critic put it, "Hope and Crosby had a wider appeal than most other comics of their day. Traditionally comedians like Abbott and Costello appealed to a male audience. These 'Road' pictures, however, managed to appeal to both sexes perhaps because they so successfully interwove the romance of girl-chasing with the glamour of fortune hunting. Also, Hope and Crosby offered a certain sex-appeal that female audiences welcomed. Of course the timing of the films worked in their favour too. The early ones were made for war-time audiences . . . people who were looking for pure escapism." As another reviewer of the day explained, "They offered a depiction of a simpler, more adventurous way of life in which two companions of nerve and whimsy could toss conformism to the winds." He compared them to a modern version of

Tom Sawyer and Huck Finn, which could well be the best comparison possible . . . like Tom and Huck, the trio of Bob and Bing and Dorothy went off in search of fun.

It wasn't until the end of the war that they came up with number four, *The Road To Utopia*. And for this film they took a small chance by tampering ever so slightly with the formula. This was a "period" piece. Although it opens with Mr. and Mrs. Chester Hooten . . . Bob and Dorothy . . . in 1945 or so, it flashed back thirty five years, to the turn of the century. The Hootens hear a voice at their front door and it turns out to be Duke Johnson . . . Bing Crosby . . . a long lost friend.

The three discuss the old days . . . and the time lapse drifts in. Dorothy is in search of a lost Alaskan gold mine that actually belonged to her father. Bob and Bing also happen to be on their way to Alaska, and by chance, they stumble across a map with directions to the same gold mine. Realizing that there is a great possibility of danger, Bob and Bing tear the map in half . . . setting up one of the gags that runs through the film of who's got the other half. When they first meet Dorothy, she's taken a job singing in a local Skagway saloon. She soon finds out that Bing has the map . . .

80

(Right) Road To Bali *(1952)*

doesn't realize it's only half . . . and manages to have it stolen by people she thinks are her friends. But no one in Skagway should be trusted, at least not when gold mines are at stake. Everybody tries to double cross everybody else, except Bob and Bing and Dorothy, and anyway, they've only got half the map most of the time. By the time they manage to rescue the other half and having heard Dorothy's story, they've sided with her. Then the two guys who originally stole the map from her father arrive on the scene. It eventually comes down to a stand-off, where Bing holds back the adversaries, allowing Bob and Dorothy to escape. And that's how they lose touch of Bing for the next 35 years.

It's all fairly silly.

The one thing that saves the film is the slew of asides. Even today they're kind of funny. For instance . . . Bob and Bing take part in an amateur talent contest and lose. Bob mumbles, "Next time I'll bring Sinatra." For instance . . . Bing shows up at Bob's place and Bob mumbles, "And I thought this was going to be an A picture." For instance . . . while crossing the great northern tundra, Bob points to a mountain and says, "Bread and butter." Crosby makes like he doesn't understand. He says, "That's a mountain." No, Hope says, "Looks like bread and butter to me." And that's when the mountain they're staring at suddenly takes on the same features as the familiar Paramount mountain shown at the opening of each of their films. For instance . . . Bob and Bing are in a ship's boiler room, working their way up to Alaska, and an extremely well dressed chap comes walking through. They wonder, "Are you in this picture?" And he tells them, "No," as he walks by, "I'm just taking a short cut to Stage 10." For instance . . . and finally . . . at various times during the film, Robert Benchley appears in a small cameo at the corner of the screen, there to explain various bits and pieces to the audience, such as, "This is a device known as a flashback."

With *The Road To Rio* three years later, they returned to the usual "Road" picture formula, and surrounded it with the famous Brazilian carnival. Bing and Bob play Scat Sweeney and Hot Lips Barton, a pair of musicians who can't manage to find work anywhere except at small town fairs. It seems they once worked regularly in Hollywood, but Scat likes ladies and is especially fond of squandering Hot Lips' money. Because they are short of funds, Scat signs Hot Lips up as a high-wire acrobat with a tent-show. They had already used the human cannon ball gag. When Hop Lips falls off his high-wire bicycle, he manages to totally wreck the show. Forced to escape the wrath of the owner, they stow away on a ship bound for Rio. Because stow-aways can't have first class cabins, they're relegated to sleeping in a life-boat. All would probably have gone smoothly for them, except that the beautiful Lucia . . . played by you know who . . . has decided to jump overboard. Scat saves her. It seems she is upset about being forced into a marriage by her nasty aunt who has been secretly hynotizing her. Not surprisingly, Scat and Lucia instantly fall in love.

Thanks to Lucia's influence, Scat and Hot Lips are permitted to leave the life-boat for better quarters, having agreed to work their way to Rio as members of the ship's orchestra. But Lucia is still in danger, as her aunt has two henchmen to watch out for her. When the ship arrives in Rio, Scat and Hot Lips smuggle Lucia ashore, enlist the help of three Brazilian musicians and form a band called the Dixie Hotshots. They get a job in a fancy nightspot, and with Lucia as the girl-singer, they become instant stars. But the nasty aunt hypnotizes Lucia into getting Scat and Hot Lips fired, then hypnotizes Scat and Hot Lips into believing that they are a pair of French counts who are about to fight a duel. However, before they kill each other, they come out of the spell, realize why Lucia has been acting so strangely, and rush off to save her from the forced marriage. Luckily, they arrive in the nick of time, hypnotize the nasty aunt, prevent the wedding, overpower the two henchmen, and save Lucia forever.

Gale Sondergaard as the nasty aunt is wonderful. But most of the critics found the film a "little light." Writing in the London *Evening Standard*, Margaret Lane felt the picture belonged to Bob Hope. "Crosby in this film does no more than expertly support and foil him (meaning Hope), and Lamour's job is simply to be the tethered lamb for the two of them to prowl around in a South American setting." Hope, she said, "had the indispensable quality, too, of touching our affections. There is something childlike in his optimism and cowardice which stirs the fondness we feel for all good clowns." Yet she added, Hope lacks "that other essential without which no funny man can indefinitely survive. He lacks good material."

A few of the gags in the film are very funny. When they come aboard the ship as stowaways, Bing is dressed like a butcher and Bob is dressed in a lamb's costume, carried onboard by Bing to be hung in a meat locker. At one point, Dorothy tells Bob, "I find myself saying things and I don't know why I say them." He suggests, "Why don't you just run for Congress and forget about us?"

But that's really about as far as it goes. Even the Paramount people must have felt that a few extra punches were needed, because *Rio* was the first of the "Road" pictures to use guest stars. The Andrews Sisters showed up in this one, and so did the Wiere Brothers. As one chronicler on the Hope and Crosby and Lamour days put it, "It appeared that the Paramount script department had run out of variations on the tripartite theme."

It took everyone five years before they could come up with another stab at that theme. This time it was *The Road To Bali*. Quoting directly from a Paramount press release which is supposed to explain the story, "Like it's five predecessors, *The Road To Bali* never makes sense at any point. The so-called plot is merely a framework on which Crosby and Hope hang their preposterous gags and at no time do they allow it to get in the way of a laugh. Designed strictly for fun, this unusual formula enables them frequently to step out of character to 'rib' each other, their friends and Hollywood. The story concerns the adventures of two

The last 'Road' movie, Road To Hong Kong *(1962)*

second-rate vaudevillians, played by Crosby and Hope, who flee Australia to avoid a pair of weddings. They meet an unscrupuious South Sea Island princess, portrayed by Murvyn Vye, who hires them to dive for sunken treasure off a mythical island somewhere on the road to Bali. This shady character eventually 'forgets' to mention one minor detail – all the other divers who have attempted to recover the fortune have been strangled to death by a giant squid."

You know by this time that before and after the giant squid battles, Dorothy Lamour appears is in distress and must be saved. You know too, who saves her.

The first of the "Road" films in colour, Hope and Crosby are making one of their fast exits, traipsing across a field of sheep. They start to sing *The Whiffenpoof Song* . . . "We are poor little lambs who have lost our way . . ." and the sheep come in as the chorus with, "Baa . . . baa . . . baa . . ." Crosby then comes out with the aside, "Fred Waring must have played through here." When Dorothy asks Bing and Bob if they always fight over women, Bing tells her yes, because "We never had any money." That's when Bob steps in with an aside to the tax collector, "That's for Washington." Never one to let his best friend off the hook, Bob waits until Bing starts singing a love song to Dorothy before he looks into the camera and tells the audiences, "Now's the time to go out and get popcorn."

Anthony Quinn showed up again in this film : . . his third as a "Road" villain . . . and he takes a shot at Bob in a diving suit. Except that Bob isn't in the diving suit. Crosby is surprised and asks Bob how he got out of it. "It was easy," Hope smiles, then pantomimes the extremely complicated escape he had to make. In the middle of it, getting back at his best friend, Bing walks over to the camera, and simply shrugs.

The best gag of all, however, has to be the one at the end. Dorothy has chosen Bing over Bob. Not one to go down without a fight, Bob takes a flute and plays it over a huge basket. Magic. Jane Russell appears. Hope figures he's won a girl of his own. But suddenly Jane Russell also chooses Bing over Bob. "What are you going to do with two girls?" He demands of Bing. The answer is, "That's my problem." Bing walks off with Dorothy and Jane. Hope panics. "THE END" sign is about to come onto the screen. "This picture isn't over yet," he screams. "Call the producer . . . call the writers . . ."

Call the critics. Unfortunately, not all of them were happy with the film. "At it's best," wrote one, "an intimate revue packed full of private jokes for picturegoers. At it's worst, it puts me in mind of a rowdy children's party, with a couple of nice uncles and a sporting auntie dressed up comical to make things go." Added another reviewer felt that the "Road" pictures have "had an inspired lunacy, an extempore air as if the songs, the gags and the story were being thought up as they went along. This planned disorganization is still the strongest point of the latest in the series, *The Road To Bali*. But the planning shows through."

Planning not only showed through *The Road To Hong Kong* . . . the seventh and last in the series . . . it also caused some hard feelings. Ten years now separated two "Road" pictures. And in 1962 when they decided to put this one together, Joan Collins was cast as the female lead, with only a very minor role left for Dorothy Lamour.

Her answer was to walk out.

As reported in the London *Sunday Express*, "The still beautiful forty-six year old actress, whose sarongs were so famous that one of them even found its way into a museum, sat hurt and angry in her New York hotel suite last night. 'I am not coming,' she told me on the phone. 'The part requires me to speak only four lines of dialogue and sing one song. During that song a chase is going on, and while I sing, fish are jumping from Hope's and Crosby's clothing. Well, I have my pride. I won't be going on this particular road.'"

She said in that interview that not being included as one of the stars for a "Road" picture was very strange to understand. "I've always thought of us as a trio." And then she admitted, "In any other picture I would take bottom billing, but not in a 'Road' film."

It turns out that when the producers first started talking about doing another "Road" picture, they didn't know what to do about Dorothy. Whether it was her age or the fact that her star had faded since the '40s no one was willing to say. But Joan Collins made a better prize for Bob and Bing to chase after, so what to do about Dorothy? As producer Melvin Frank told the press, "We realized we didn't dare make the film without her. So for old time's sake we gave her a part which, though small, helps resolve the plot."

It was a pretty weak excuse. And looking back, not including Dorothy Lamour as one of the stars of a 'Road' picture seems fairly poor taste. Luckily Dorothy Lamour swallowed her pride and made the film. It just wouldn't have been a 'Road' picture without her.

Unfortunately, it wasn't much of a picture, even with her. It's all too contrived, and the Hope-Crosby-Lamour magic doesn't happen when the team gets changed to Hope-Crosby-Collins.

Harry and Chester . . . Bob and Bing . . . are ex-vaudevillians who happen to be in Ceylon selling Do-It-Yourself Space Kits. When a demonstration of the kit fails, Chester suffers from amnesia, which means he can't remember where he's hidden their money. The only person who can help restore Chester's memory is the Grand Lama in Tibet. But on the way, Diane The Secret Agent . . . played by Joan Collins . . . mistakes Chester for her contact and slips a stolen Russian rocket fuel formula into his pocket. The Grand Lama gives Chester herbs to cure his amnesia, but they get mixed up with tea at about the same time that Diane and her superiors of "The Third Echelon" are trying to get the formula back from him. When all looks bleakest for Harry and Chester, Diane decides she's in love with the boys, and attempts to save them. By this time they're in Hong Kong, racing through the crowded streets, until they barge into a club where Dorothy Lamour is singing. "I'd better hide you," she says. Bing asks, "From the killers?'' She says, 'No, from the critics.'' Too bad she couldn't manage just that. Bob and Bing and Joan get trapped in one of the do-it-yourself spaceships, and are blasted off into space, where they finally land on Plutonius and, as the only humans there, must live happily ever after.

Put bluntly, the era of the ''Road'' films was long gone. By the '60s the nature of film comedy had changed. Television had taken over from radio, and sit-coms everynight/all night were turning the American public into an audience who wanted a certain brand of humour . . . *Bilko, The Beverly Hillbillies, The Dick Van Dyke Show* . . . not vaudeville, not radio, something particularly television-esque. The ''Road'' pictures no longer stood a chance. Yet in spite of it, at the time of Bing Crosby's death on a Spanish golf course, there was serious talk going around Hollywood that the trio would indeed give it yet another try . . . *The Road To The Fountain Of Youth*. Perhaps it's best that the film was never made. In cases like this, it might be best to simply remember the road-bound threesome when they and the gags were both much younger.

The Films Of Hope, Crosby and Lamour

The Road To Singapore – 1940 – Paramount
The Road To Zanzibar – 1941 – Paramount
The Road To Morocco – 1942 – Paramount
The Road To Utopia – 1945 – Paramount
The Road To Rio – 1948 – Paramount
The Road To Bali – 1952 – Paramount
The Road To Hong Kong – 1962 – United Artists

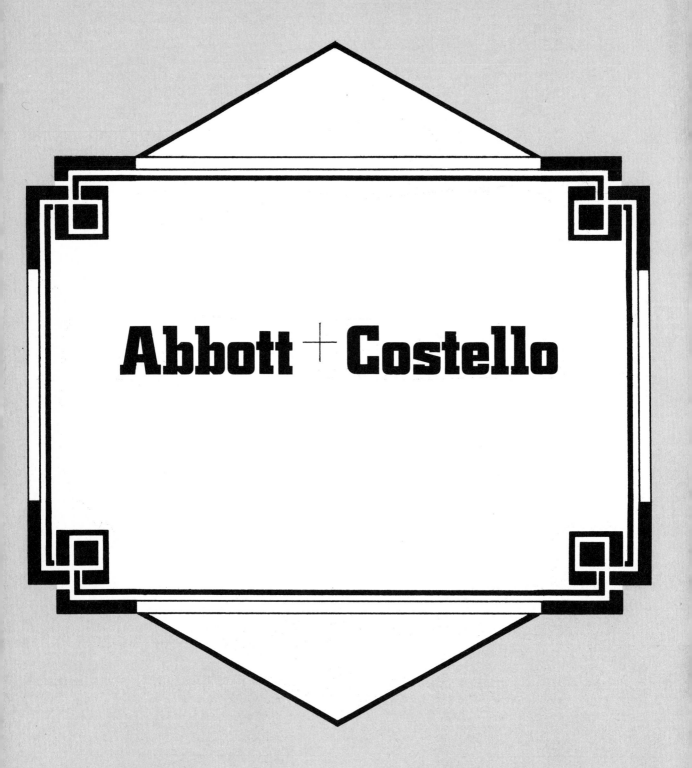

Abbott + Costello

Bud Abbott and Lou Costello with Nina of the Dancing Theodores in their first film, One Night In The Tropics *(1940)*

They were strictly burlesque, and that worked so well on radio that someone started wondering if it would also work in the movies. No need to worry much about things like plot. Just stick them in the middle of the set . . . maybe dress them up in some sort of costume so at least they look like they belong in the film . . . and let them do their routine. Let them do it word for word, the same way they used to do it on stage, four shows a day, five on Saturdays, more on holidays.

The film was *One Night In The Tropics*, starring Allan Jones, Robert Cummings, Nancy Kelly and Mary Boland. The cast alone should tell you how memorable it is. Songs were actually written by Jerome Kern with lyrics by Oscar Hammerstein and Dorothy Fields. Go ahead and whistle any one of them! The plot had something to do with the tropics. Abbott and Costello were hired to do a burlesque routine in the middle of the film, even if the storyline didn't necessarily call for a burlesque routine. Someone somewhere was hedging a bet. Abbott and Costello had just scored big on Broadway so why not stick them into a film just in case the film is going to be a flop. Might as well make sure there's something funny in it.

The director was A. Edward Sutherland. Born in England, his claim to fame in Hollywood was as a former Keystone Cop at the Sennett Studio. Without any knowledge of stand-up comedy or burlesque routines, he probably wondered what Abbott and Costello were doing in this film. When they came onto the set for their very first movie together, neither Bud nor Lou really had any idea what anyone wanted of them, except a burlesque routine. So they did their act. But to everyone's confusion, whenever Sutherland would yell out to set up another shot, they'd have to start their routine again from the beginning. Being interrupted like that baffled them. Starting over again baffled everyone else.

Somewhere around the halfway point of the shooting schedule, Sutherland, the writers and the producers realized that Abbott and Costello were funny enough to be more than talking clowns plunked down into this film. They rewrote some scenes and reshot wherever they could, making Bud and Lou's appearance correspond as well as possible with the already mixed up plot of the film. *One Night In The Tropics* still turned out to be a fairly terrible movie, but something quite unexpected came out of it. Bud and Lou were instant movie stars. Universal signed them with Hollywood's first percentage deal . . . they were on for 10% of their films . . . and after four films, Abbott and Costello were millionaires.

Bud Abbott's real first name was William, and he was born in New Jersey in 1895. His parents had both worked for the Barnum and Bailey Circus, and if Bud's straightman career was built around a "carney barker" type of character, it obviously came from the people he saw whilst growing up. By the time he finished high school his parents had given up their circus lives and were in the management side of burlesque. It meant that Bud got to see just about every act in the country

. . . they all came through his father's theatre . . . and the more he saw of burlesque the more he knew that he was a natural straight man.

It's not an easy job. Being a comic's foil requires talent and skill, timing and a thorough knowledge of the comic's thought pattern so that the routine doesn't go astray. That's one of the reasons why the straight man was usually higher paid than the clown. Bud was bright, learned routines quickly, and talented enough to be a first rate straight man. Before very long, he was one of the best in the business and always in demand as a partner.

Lou's real name was Louis Francis Cristillo, and he was also born in New Jersey, some eleven years after Bud. His father was an Italian immigrant. His mother was half Italian, half Irish. There was no theatre background anywhere in the family, and anyway, the theatre was not where Lou thought he was headed. He would have liked to play pro basketball. He played the game well enough, but he was only 5 ft 4 in. He boxed well, but Lou's father had other ideas about that kind of a career for his son. He always liked the movies, so he decided one day, why not become a movie star. Everybody told him he was funny enough. It seemed like a good idea.

At twenty one years of age, Lou Cristillo with a friend in tow, hopped a freight train smoking west. Thinking Cristillo wasn't a name worthy of a film star, he changed it to Costello for no reason except that he thought it sounded better. Unfortunately, Lou Costello was quickly disillusioned with Hollywood. The closest he came to stardom was as a part time stuntman. Adding insult to injury, because of his size, he was most often asked to double stunts for women. The height of his career was pretending to be Dolores Del Rio in *The Trail Of '98*, and Joan Crawford in *Taxi Dancer*.

Out of luck and money, he decided to come back east. But the pal he had gone to Hollywood with had relatives in Missouri and they figured if they could only get that far they'd have some place to stay for a while. Once they arrived in Missouri, Lou somehow convinced a local theatre manager to hire him as a comic. He lied about having all sorts of stage experience, got the job and found he could make people laugh doing pratfalls, the way he learned them as a stuntman. By 1936, Lou Costello was one of the comic stars of the burlesque circuit.

What happened next comes in many different versions. Even Bud and Lou themselves have told different stories about how they came to team up. In one version, Lou's straightman didn't make it to the show and Bud stepped in at the last minute. In another, it was Bud who helped bail Lou out of a gambling debt and this was Lou's way of paying him back. What probably happened was that both of them found themselves stymied by their then partners and were both in the market for a new one. It was in New York in 1936 that they met, saw each other's act, and decided they'd be better off together. They toured with *Life Begins At Minsky's* and, by 1938 were breaking box office records

everywhere. The singer Kate Smith featured them on her nation-wide CBS radio programme . . . supposedly at $1250 a show . . . and within weeks, America's children were all doing their imitations of Abbott and Costello and "Who's On First?"

Lou wants to know the names of the players on the St. Louis team, so Bud tells him, "Who's on first, What's on second. I Don't Know's on third."

"That's what I want to find out," Lou says. "I want you to tell me the names of the fellows on the St. Louis team."

"I'm telling you," Bud insists. "Who's on first. What's on second. I Don't Know's on third."

Confused, Lou asks, "You know the fellows' names?"

"Yes."

"Well, then, who's playing first?"

"Yes."

"I mean," Lou says, "the fellow's name on first base."

Bud tells him, "Who."

"The fellow playing first base for St. Louis."

Again Bud says, "Who."

Lou says, "The guy on first base."

Bud tries to make him understand. "Who is on first base."

Lou screams, "Well, what are you asking me for?"

"I'm not asking you," Bud says, "I'm telling you. Who is on first."

"I'm asking you. Who's on first?"

"That's the man's name."

"That's whose name?"

"Yes," says Bud.

Lou can't figure it out. "Well, go ahead and tell me."

"Who."

"The guy on first."

"Who."

"The first baseman."

"Who is on first."

Now Lou decides to try it another way. "Have you got a first baseman on first?"

"Certainly," says Bud.

Lou shakes his head. "Then who's playing first?"

Bud agrees. "Absolutely."

Lou tries another approach. "When you pay off the first baseman every month, who gets the money?"

"Every dollar of it," Bud says. "And why not, the man's entitled to it."

It's perhaps THE classic Abbott and Costello routine. "What's the guy's name on first base?" Lou wonders. Bud explains, "No. What is on second base." When Bud repeats, "Who's on first," Lou says, "I don't know," and Bud has to explain, "He's on third. We're not talking about him." Lou wants to know the pitcher's name and Bud tells him, "Tomorrow." Lou insists, "Today," and Bud says, "He's the catcher."

It worked well enough on *The Kate Smith Hour* to make them national stars. When they made the Universal picture *The Naughty Nineties*, they simply took it word for word and put it into the script. If there is any formula to their films, that's it. They stuck with

what they knew was funny.

Their success on radio brought them to Broadway and the legitimate theatre, as stars of *The Streets Of Paris*. It was a revue that featured, among others, Carmen Miranda. But it was Bud and Lou who got the rave notices from the New York Times. "They belong to the traditional school of mountebanks that pairs a dazed clown with an abusive straight man . . ." And the show ran for 274 performances.

That success took them to Hollywood.

The film that immediately followed *One Night In The Tropics* was the result of sound logic. It was 1941. War was just around the corner. The United States was getting ready to do battle and young men were being drafted into the army. For Abbott and Costello's first film as stars, they made *Buck Privates*.

Bud and Lou get drafted. Somewhere along the line it seems as if the Andrews Sisters have gotten drafted also. They sing *Apple Blossom Time, You're A Lucky Fellow Mr. Smith,* and how's this for trivia, *The Boogie-Woogie Bugle Boy Of Company B*. Lee Bowman and Alan Curtis vie for the affections of June Frazee. But it seems the only reason anyone else is in the film, besides Bud and Lou, is to be something of an intermission for their burlesque routines which they now do in Army costumes.

Abbott is Smitty. Costello is Herbie. Smitty is always conniving. Herbie is always falling for it. Smitty tries to borrow $50 but Herbie says no because all he has is $40. "All right," Smitty says, "give me forty dollars and you owe me ten."

"Okay," Herbie says, "I owe you ten."

"All right."

But then Herbie wonders, "How come I owe you ten?"

"What did I ask you for?"

"Fifty dollars."

"And how much did you give me?"

"Forty dollars."

"So? You owe me ten dollars."

"That's right," Herbie says, "but you owe me forty."

And now Smitty warns, "Don't change the subject."

The routine goes back and forth until Smitty has divested Herbie of all his money, much the same way he did a few reels earlier when the two of them did their "Crap Game" routine. Smitty gets Herbie's last ten dollars by making a bet with him that he can't guess the number he's got in mind. He instructs Herbie to choose a number from one to ten and not say which.

Herbie nods, "I got it."

Smitty asks, "Is the number odd or even?"

"Even."

"Is the number between one and three?"

"No."

"Between three and five."

"No," Herbie says confidently. "I think I've got him."

"Is it between five and seven?"

Herbie says, "Yeah."

Smitty points at him. "Number six," he announces.

Lou Costello in Lost In A Harem *(1944)*

Africa Screams (*1949*)

"Right," Herbie says, then tries to figure out the trick. "How did he do that?"

Throughout the film Lou runs up against his sergeant, played by Nat Pendleton, a familiar face in Abbott and Costello films. He was a cop or a sergeant or a Navy chief, some sort of authority figure around whom Bud and Lou would have to manoeuvre. Bud would con Lou into making the move, and invariably Lou would wind up running right into Pendleton. In *Buck Privates* he makes the mistake of throwing some water towards the door of his tent, and just then Pendleton walks in. "You," Pendleton shouts, "I'll strangle you." Herbie panics and runs to the far end of the tent, shaking in fear with, "Oh, I'm a very b-a-a-a-a-d boy."

That line became so popular, that at least one generation of young American children, if not two, used it to try and talk their mothers out of a spanking.

The tremendous success of *Buck Privates* suggested to the Hollywood powers that they had the right idea. So, if it worked once, it ought to work again. The key question was, how?

Universal came up with a film called *Hold That Ghost*, in which Abbott and Costello fulfilled the promise of the title . . . that is, when not doing burlesque routines. The cast included the Ink Spots, Tip-Tap-and-Toe, Jack La Rue, and Sharkey the Seal. Every haunted house gag on earth gets used in this film. But just before it was to be released, someone at the studio realized that it might not be the perfect vehicle to follow *Buck Privates*. They put *Hold That Ghost* on the shelf, to be sent out to the public after effort number three, a take-off on *Buck Privates* that was called *In The Navy*. This time, instead of Lee Bowman playing the romantic lead, they used Dick Powell. But the Andrews Sisters were now in the Navy. So was Shemp Howard, one of the Three Stooges.

Just as privates in the Army need money . . . and Abbott and Costello did some of their money routines in that film . . . so do sailors . . . and so Abbott and Costello do more money routines.

There's one where Bud counts the change he's giving Lou for a ten dollar bill. He hands over one dollar, then a second, then asks Lou how many years he's been in the Navy. Lou says six. Bud says six, then counts the next bill as seven, then eight, and so forth. Lou thinks he's been cheated, but can't quite figure it out. He decides to try it on the chef in the mess hall, sets it up and then asks the chef how long he's been in the Navy. The chef says, ninety days. Totally baffling for Lou. Very funny for the audience.

Bud then slips into the "Lemon" routine, a variation on a game known as "3-card Monty". In other circles it's just "The Shell Game". Doing it exactly the way they used to do it on the burlesque stage, Bud puts a lemon under three cups and whirls them across a table. Of course, the table has a hole in it and there's a basket under the table where the lemons collect. Lou eventually catches Bud cheating, at which time the joke turns around. Bud gives Lou a shot at it, and of course, Lou fumbles the ball.

He gets his revenge, however, in this film when he proves beyond any reasonable doubt that seven times thirteen equals twenty-eight. It all has to do with the doughnuts Lou is making while on K.P. Because there are twenty-eight doughnuts in all, each of the seven officers will be allowed to eat thirteen of the doughnuts. Bud claims that's ridiculous because everyone knows that seven times four is twenty-eight. Lou shows him it's not, using a very roundabout method to multiply seven times three, equalling twenty-one, then seven times one . . . the one in front of the three which means thirteen . . . to make seven, then adding twenty-one and seven to come up with twenty-eight. When Bud suggests that Lou write the number thirteen seven times and add it up, Lou does it the same way. All those threes add up to twenty-one. All those ones add up to seven. Twenty-one plus seven is twenty-eight. And as he proves it, he gloats with a smugness worthy only of a man who has succeeded, even if he hasn't.

Now that the formula incorporated into a military background had worked so well twice, why not a third time? This time they called the same film they had already made with the Army and the Navy, *Keep 'Em Flying*. The Andrews Sisters didn't make this one, but Martha Raye did, and she almost played a love scene with Lou. He invites her into the Tunnel of Love. "We could have a lot of fun in there. We'd get in a boat all by ourselves, and when we got to a place where it was dark and nobody could see us . . ." She cut in with, "Then what would we do?" And Lou answered, "We could take off our shoes and put our feet in the water!"

This is also the film where Bud and Lou do their "half a sandwich" routine, the same one Laurel and Hardy used with ice cream sodas in *Men O' War*. And again, the difference between the two teams is easily seen with this routine. Where Stan Laurel slowly comes to understand that he is supposed to refuse the soda because they don't have enough money, Lou Costello is more obstinate in asking for a sandwich. Where Babe Hardy politely excuses himself to explain to Stan why he must refuse the soda, Bud Abbott is rougher with Lou, grabbing him to make him refuse the sandwich.

Picture number five was a western . . . again a slight plot written around a series of burlesque gags . . . complete with a cast that included Johnny Mack Brown, and famous cowgirl star, Ella Fitzgerald. By this time the United States had entered the war, and the market for film comedies had never been riper. A country at war is a country that wants to laugh. The main sketch in this film was "The Crazy House," where cowboy Lou decides to take a nap, while around him there are cowboys and Indians fighting it out. For some strange reason there is even a swami who happens by, asks Lou if he'd like his palm read, and when Lou says sure, he paints it red.

The second phase of their film career now clicked into gear. They left Universal and went to MGM where they did *Rio Rita* with a singing Kathryn Grayson. But Universal lured them back for five more films, now bigger budget affairs than the first five, and three of those films contain truly classic Abbott and Costello routines. In *It Ain't Hay* they do their "Mudder" gag. One of the race track punters is explaining to Lou how to read a scratch sheet. He says, "If a horse has an X in front of his name, that shows he's a mudder."

Lou doesn't understand. "How can he be a mudder. Ain't a she always a mudder?"

Now Bud tries to explain. "No. Sometimes a he is a better mudder than a she."

"A he makes a better mudder than a she?" Lou can't believe it. "How can you tell if a horse is a mudder."

"By looking at its feet," Bud says.

Lou looks up to the heavens. "Ain't we living in a wonderful age? Whoo. Mudder . . . Fodder . . ."

In *Hit The Ice* they do exactly the same routine, but this time the word is teller, as in someone who works in a bank. "Teller," Bud calls out as they walk into the bank.

Lou wants to know, "Tell who?"

"Teller," Bud repeats.

"I'll tell her," Lou says. "Where is she?"

"Where is who? I said 'teller'."

"Tell her what?"

"Tell her nothing. I want the teller."

"Well go ahead and tell her, I don't care."

"No," Bud shouts, "teller in a bank."

Lou shrugs, "Tell her in a bank. Tell her outside. Tell her any place you want. I won't listen."

Finally for the film *In Society* they do what used to be known in burlesque as a "cross-over". And the routine is called "Beagle Street". It might even rival "Who's on First" as being their funniest.

As hat salesmen they've got to deliver some hats to a company on Beagle Street, except that they don't know where it is. They decide to ask someone. Bud makes sure it's Lou who does the asking.

The first man who comes along gets asked where Beagle Street is, and he answers that he doesn't have any money to give to beggars. Lou says he doesn't want money, he only wants to know if the man knows where Beagle Street is. The man then goes into a very long and aggressive speech, saying sure he knows where Beagle Street is because he was born on Beagle Street and so was his brother born on Beagle Street and, "Do you know my brother? What right have you got to go around talking about my brother?" The man continues, giving Lou nothing more to do than come up with a series of expressions to show how uncomfortable he is. When Lou finally manages to get a word in edgewise, telling the man that all he wants is directions to the Susquehanna Hat Company on Beagle Street, the man sets off on another long tirade about how that particular hat company is using child labour. He then takes one of the hats Lou and Bud are to deliver, punches a hole in the top of it, then beats Lou on the head with it a few times, before storming off.

Lou as the victim turns to Bud, who has no sympathy because the hat has been damaged and it's obviously Lou who's going to have to pay for it.

Next comes a lady walking by, and when Lou asks her how to find Beagle Street, she breaks into tears. It

seems her husband was killed on Beagle Street, and he was wearing a hat just like the kind Lou has. She takes her vengeance out on the hat, and she too goes off down the block.

That's two hats ruined, and no directions to Beagle Street.

Bud warns him to stop insulting women, and find out fast where Beagle Street is. Another woman comes along, Lou asks and the woman screams, "Beagle Street. Don't ever mention that name." A third hat gets ripped to shreds.

Now a man happens past, and when Lou asks him where Beagle Street is, he starts to cry that he was killed on Beagle Street when a safe fell from a fifteen storey building. Totally confused, Lou figures, "Then, as long as you're dead, there's no use asking you where the Susquehanna Hat Company is."

"Susquehanna Hat Company?" the dead man shrieks. "That's the hat I was wearing the day I was killed."

Hat number four is destroyed. In the ruckus a friend of Lou's named Luigi happens along, calls the police and saves Lou from the man who claims to have been killed in a Susquehanna Hat. When Lou explains to Luigi that he's merely looking for the Susquehanna Hat Company on Beagle Street, Luigi shouts, "Susquehanna. Susquehanna." And promptly takes an axe to everything in sight.

Needless to say, Bud and Lou never get to Beagle Street.

By the time the war was over they had made a total of sixteen films together, including *One Night In The Tropics*, which meant they had starred in fifteen. Some critics say that by this time they had made their best films. They did a pair of pictures in 1946 . . . *Little Giant* and *The Time Of Their Lives* . . . in both of which they did not appear as a team. And while the films were interesting, it started to become obvious that Abbott was a great straight man but hardly an actor, and Costello was a very funny fellow but one who needed a straight man.

That's when everything started to turn sour.

Their partnership had suffered ups and downs before, but as successes had piled up so fast, it put a strain on their friendship. Lou became very demanding of Bud, even to the point of suggesting that the team change their name to Costello and Abbott. Bud refused. Lou demanded that the money split 60-40 in his

favour and even though Bud tried to refuse, Costello put him in a position where he finally had to give in. Their egos began to get the best of them. Their films began to suffer.

They groped in the dark with *Buck Privates Come Home,* trying to find something that once was. Keep the plot simple and string burlesque routines along into the semblance of a movie. It had worked before, it could work again. But the audience had now heard a lot of their routines . . . there was an Abbott and Costello radio programme where they used them . . . and a routine, no matter how funny, wasn't going to stay funny if it was overused.

They hit on the idea of *Abbott And Costello Meet . . .* and filled in the blanks with *Frankenstein,* then *Boris Karloff,* then *The Invisible Man,* then *Captain Kydd,* then *Dr. Jekyll And Mr. Hyde,* Then *The Keystone Cops,* and then finally, *The Mummy.* It was, like those earlier films, a series that worked off a formula. And when you think of putting Charles Laughton into an Abbott and Costello film . . . he played Captain Kydd . . . that in itself is a funny idea. Karloff played himself in the film where they meet him. Lon Chaney and Bela Lugosi worked with the two in the Frankenstein picture. But it just wasn't enough. There were too many inconsistencies. The films were too often silly instead of funny.

They tried television, and reworked their old burlesque gags there because a new generation was growing up. But even that didn't work as well as it might have. The older the two got, the more the bad blood flowed between them. Their last picture was called *Dance With Me Henry.* It's a shame they even bothered.

Right afterwards, they officially split up. Bud Abbott tried to retire. Lou Costello tried to keep working. Neither succeeded at what they were doing. Bud was broke and had to look for work. Lou was alone and no matter who stood next to him on a Las Vegas stage or in a television appearance, the world knew it wasn't Bud. Lou made a low budget film for Columbia with Dorothy Provine called *The Thirty Foot Bride Of Candy Rock,* but the magic was long gone. His health was failing as well. And before that film could be released, Lou Costello died of a heart attack, on March 3, 1959.

Bud Abbott survived him by fifteen years. He worked a little . . . there just wasn't a lot he could do . . . and jumped at the chance to dub his own voice on to a series of two hundred Abbott and Costello cartoons made by the Hanna-Barbera team in 1967. But putting his own voice on a cartoon production wasn't an ego trip for him – he desperately needed the money. He died almost penniless in 1974.

Abbott And Costello Go To Mars *(1953)*

The Films Of Abbott And Costello

One Night In The Tropics – 1940 – Universal
Buck Privates – 1941 – Universal
Hold That Ghost – 1941 – Universal
In The Navy – 1941 – Universal
Keep 'Em Flying – 1941 – Universal
Ride 'Em Cowboy – 1942 – Universal
Rio Rita – 1942 – MGM
Pardon My Sarong – 1942 – Universal
Who Done It? – 1942 – Universal
It Ain't Hay – 1943 – Universal
Hit The Ice – 1943 – Universal
In Society – 1944 – Universal
Lost In A Harem – 1944 – MGM
The Naughty Nineties – 1945 – Universal
Abbott And Costello In Hollywood – 1945 – MGM
Here Come The Co-Eds – 1945 – Universal
Little Giant – 1946 – Universal
The Time Of Their Lives – 1946 – Universal
Buck Privates Come Home – 1947 – Universal
The Wistful Widow Of Wagon Gap – 1947 – Universal
The Noose Hangs High – 1948 – Eagle Lion
Abbott And Costello Meet Frankenstein – 1948 – Universal

Mexican Hayride – 1948 – Universal
Abbott And Costello Meet The Killer, Boris Karloff – 1949 – Universal
Africa Screams – 1949 – Nassour-UA
Abbott And Costello In The Foreign Legion – 1950 – Universal
Abbott And Costello Meet The Invisible Man – 1951 – Universal
Comin' Round The Mountain – 1951 – Universal
Jack And The Beanstalk – 1952 – Warner Brothers
Lost In Alaska – 1952 – Universal
Abbott And Costello Meet Captain Kydd – 1953 – Warner Brothers
Abbott And Costello Go To Mars – 1953 – Universal
Abbott And Costello Meet Dr. Jekyll And Mr. Hyde – 1953 – Universal
Abbott And Costello Meet The Keystone Cops – 1955 – Universal
Abbott And Costello Meet The Mummy – 1955 – Universal
Dance With Me, Henry – 1956 – United Artists

Martin + Lewis

An entire generation has now grown up and started to beget a second generation who think of Jerry Lewis only as the zany perennial kid, the star of late night films like *The Nutty Professor*, *The Sad Sack* and *Don't Give Up The Ship*. And, of course, the man who does annual weekend telethons to raise money for charity. The French are so crazy about Jerry Lewis that they invite him regularly to star in their hallowed music hall L'Olympia where he sings and clowns and pretends to be typing to the tune of *Typewriter*. They even publish long and slightly tiresome articles about him in French cinema magazines, explaining his particular genius. But in the States, except for his telethons, he is not the household name he once was.

That same generation thinks of Dean Martin as the handsome crooner who jokes about drinking and does television specials with Frank Sinatra. He too starred in films that pop up on the Late Show, but some of them are minor classics. *The Young Lions*, *Some Came Running*, *Rio Bravo*, *The Sons Of Katie Elder* and *Airport*. He's not only made more films than Jerry Lewis, he's also had a whole slew of high rating television seasons. On top of that, as a single, his act is one of the all-time highest paid affairs in Las Vegas.

Where Lewis is forever the child-clown, Martin has matured into the epitome of a modern entertainer. But it wasn't always like this, and none of it came easily. The success they both have today . . . the good and the bad . . . is the result of nearly thirty-five years of earning it. Yet had they never met and teamed up, it's possible that neither of them would be anything today.

They came into the world ten years and a thousand miles apart. In 1917, Dean Martin was born Dino Paul Crocetti. The place was Steubenville, Ohio, a factory town not far from Pittsburgh. As a kid who didn't necessarily care for school, Dino dropped out at the age of fifteen to bounce around a bunch of odd-jobs until he found one working in a backroom casino, running a craps table. Because he could do a fair imitation of Bing Crosby's style, he eventually wound up vocalizing with a local band, and that led to a better spot with a band in "big time" Cleveland. It was wartime and so a lot of talent from the stage was off somewhere fighting or, at least, entertaining the troops. The Crocetti kid, now working under the name of Dean Martin, found it less difficult to get bookings than he might otherwise have in peacetime. He worked steadily throughout the war years in spite of the fact that reviews of his performances were generally less than raves. "Lacking in personality," wrote someone in Variety when Dean first played New York. "Looks ill-fitting in that dinner jacket and at best, has just a fair voice." At one point some talent scout saw him and sent his name out west, but the moguls weren't interested. They had Tony Martin signed to a contract and the response came back, "Who wants another Italian singer." It was a wonderful answer, seeing as how Tony Martin isn't Italian. Anyway, had Dean gone west . . . meaning that he wouldn't have met Jerry Lewis . . . his career might never have taken off. As it was he met Lewis

while working in New York in 1945, and the two became friends. But friendship with another performer was one thing. Giving a single minute's thought to how the next ten years might change both of their lives was something totally different. It wouldn't be for nearly 20 years that Dean would say in an interview, "Two of the greatest turning points in my career were, first, meeting Jerry Lewis, second, leaving Jerry Lewis."

In 1926, Jerry Lewis was born Joseph Levitch. The place was Newark, New Jersey, a factory town across the Hudson River from New York. In those days Newark was certainly as bleak a place as Steubenville. With parents in vaudeville, Joseph was "born in a trunk" and, at times during his youth, he sang on stage with his mother and father. He too dropped out of school early on, and bounced around various jobs, working for a while as an usher in a New York theatre, then as a busboy in a Catskill Mountains' resort hotel. But right from the start he knew he was a naturally funny kid, could make faces to get laughs, and figured show business was where he should be. He put together an act, lip-syncing records. He'd stand on a stage with a record of someone singing opera, and he'd mouth the words, mime and grimace. Most of his audiences in those very early days sat still for a couple of minutes then began demanding that the kid comic get lost so that the strippers could come back.

Somehow towards the end of the war, now working as Jerry Lewis because Lewis was the name his parents had used, he got himself booked into a New York club. When he and Martin became friends, he felt it would be funny to tease his friend. He'd show up at the club where Martin was singing, pretend to be a waiter, come walking down the aisle and suddenly drop a tray full of dishes. Martin laughed. The audience loved it. And that was all there was supposed to be. A little impromptu fun. Jerry never gave a minute's thought as to how that clowning could change both of their lives.

Then came 1946. Today there are several variations on the story, many of them suggesting that it was Jerry Lewis who helped save Dean's career by inviting him to work on the same stage at the Club 500 in Atlantic City, New Jersey. It's likely, however, that isn't quite the way it happened. In *Everybody Loves Somebody Sometime*, the extremely well written account of the Martin and Lewis partnership by Arthur Marx . . . Groucho's son . . . the story is different. Marx suggests that Jerry Lewis was about to be fired at the Club 500 because nobody cared for his lip-sync act. With a wife and baby to feed, he rang Dean's agent in desperation asking for help. When help arrived, it was Dean who sang while Jerry did the plate dropping routine. From there they built onto the act, yelling, screaming, chasing each other around the room, cutting off people's ties, squirting each other, and even the audience, with seltzer bottles, and generally causing such confusion that they became instant Atlantic City stars. When word spread to Philadelphia and New York, they found themselves as much an over-night success as anyone ever did in show business.

For the first few years they remained in nightclubs.

Jerry Lewis, Corinne Calvet, Dean Martin and John Lund in My Friend Irma Goes West *(1950)*

But then they started making moves towards radio and television. America in those days was a country just discovering the power of television, and once the pair hit the tube, their success was huge.

Everything seemed to happen quickly, almost at the same time. When Hollywood fell into place the union seemed secure. It was 1948. Hal Wallis saw Martin and Lewis working in a Hollywood nightspot and signed them immediately to a five year contract. He took a chance on them because they absolutely broke him up. He had no idea whether or not they could act, but they were so funny that he wanted them to make seven films over the next five years at a salary of $50,000 per film. It doesn't sound like a lot of money today, now that Hollywood is a seven figure town, but in 1948 a man making just one-tenth of that a year could support a family. Because both Dean and Jerry were fairly careless with money in the beginning, they found that they still had to work clubs. Somehow they got Wallis to up their contract to $75,000 per film, signed on to a regular radio show with NBC, and the year after that made the move to television. Their first appearance as the hosts of NBC's *Colgate Comedy Hour* earned them $25,000. But as they were such an enormous hit, their drawing power gave them the weight to demand three times that for their next appearance. And they got it.

Yet as far as Hal Wallis was concerned he couldn't afford to risk an entire picture on them so, for their first picture *My Friend Irma,* they only got fifth and sixth billing.

Based on a popular radio series, Dean and Jerry were originally supposed to be the boyfriends of the stars, Marie Wilson and Diana Lynn. But while Dean might have had the appeal of a romantic lead, Jerry's goofy-kid didn't fit the role as defined by the radio series. In fact it seems that at one point there was talk of dropping Jerry from the picture, just using Dean and hoping a better vehicle would come around for the duo's debut. That didn't sit well with Jerry, or Dean for that matter, so the scriptwriters got together and wrote in a part for Jerry as Dean's partner in a fresh fruit juice stand.

To properly introduce Martin and Lewis to the moving going public, the Paramount Studios press office sent out a release so filled with smarm and nonsense that they couldn't possibly have done it with a straight face.

"Paramount Brings You A Great New Comedy Team," the headline read. "Filmgoers who have yearned for a brand new screen comedy team will greatly welcome the appearance of Dean Martin and Jerry Lewis, who make their film debut in Hal Wallis's *My Friend Irma* for Paramount release. These boys are probably the weirdest, the freshest, the merriest and the 'zaniest' comedy team in show business. Exponents of all the best elements in comedy, satirical as well as slapstick, they have the added attribute of 'good taste'. There has never been one risqué or 'off-colour' routine in their repertoire."

It's possible the press office had never seen Martin and Lewis on a stage. But now with middle-America reassured, the release went on to say, "The gags and

103

antics expounded by Martin and Lewis are as spontaneous and exciting as champagne bubbles. They work without the benefit of script or writers. Their humour emanates from bright, observant minds, their own! In wit and ebullience, they are 'naturals!'"

Dean Martin, they said, "Is ostensibly the straight man. At the same time, he is able, through subtle drollery, to send audiences into near-hysterics. When singing, however, he has a rich baritone voice, and if Lewis were not such a great clown, one might object to his breaking up Martin's singing with his antics." As it was, Martin started objecting before too long. The release also promised, "The act also contains several popular ballads, impersonations, skits and general upheaval. Since there is no prepared material, the boys do a great deal of ad-libbing, often surprising each other.

In spite of the Paramount press office, Dean and Jerry were a hit in *My Friend Irma*. As Dean put it several years later, "We were supposed to be proprietors of a fruit juice stand, and I guess the audiences liked the way we squeezed oranges."

If it was good once, it was good twice. Wallis cast them in the sequel, *My Friend Irma Goes West*. Believe it or not, the reviews were actually better than Wallis' press releases, and that film was immediately followed by *At War With The Army*. This time Dean and Jerry were the stars. Dean plays the sergeant. Jerry plays the private. Dean wants to chase girls and sing to them. Jerry is a goofy-kid who can't do anything right . . . he can't even get one bottle of soda out of the Coke machine. He puts his money in and Cokes start shooting out at him.

With this third film, Jerry's character was firmly established. He would forever be the likable *schnook*. Dean's character was pretty well cemented too. As far as the team of Martin and Lewis was concerned, Dean was the straightman. It was part of the formula they used, and one that made them major stars. The public couldn't get enough. And the critics liked them too. "The tomfoolery of Martin and Lewis is just as effective on the screen as on the nightclub platform," wrote the *Hollywood Reporter*. "Lewis is a rare comic whose sense of the ridiculous is simply sublime. Martin sings a lot and clicks with every number."

Variety agreed. They described Jerry Lewis as "a socko comedian," but Dean as "a straightman singer." The *New York Times* raved about Jerry, then gave Dean good marks for having "Genuine comic ability" . . . before going back to talk about Jerry Lewis again. And the *Los Angeles Examiner* felt that Jerry, "All but steals win, place and show money," adding, "There just hasn't been anything like him ever on land, sea or celluloid." As for Dean they wrote, "He shouldn't oughtta listen to any more Bing Crosby records."

Not only was the formula set for their film characters, but it seems the die might have been cast with the critics as well. They were a very funny team, but Jerry was the funny one and Dean was just hanging along for the ride.

Obviously it was a situation that didn't exactly please Dean Martin.

Of all the reviewers during those early days, it seems only one was even slightly critical of the fun Martin and Lewis were selling. That was Milton Shulman in England, who write in 1951, "In more enlightened times it would be considered impolite, almost indecent to be amused by such ugliness, lunacy and deformity." He decided that as a comedy team, Martin and Lewis "Represent a deterioration in humorous taste not far removed from what might be expected if the printing press were to be abolished or if Atilla the Hun recon-

At War With The Army (1951)

Jerry Lewis in drag with Dewey Robinson in
At War With The Army

quered Europe."

With three films making the rounds of America's movie houses, Martin and Lewis lashed out again at television, radio and nightclubs. They worked non-stop. And they made a pile of money. It would take a lot of years, however, before either of them would learn how to keep it.

In 1951, perhaps the best of all the Martin and Lewis pictures was released – *That's My Boy*. Following the formula, Jerry played the goofy son of an all-American football hero. Dean played the college football star who can be counted on to score the winning touch down, chase girls and sing to them. Yet in a very real way, this film was something of a departure for Jerry because it was the first time he was required to act. Funny faces wouldn't carry this picture. He actually had to build a believable character. It took a lot of work, but to the surprise of most people who knew him, Jerry managed it. And the success of *That's My Boy* was probably one of the nails in the coffin of Abbott and Costello's career. Martin and Lewis were the biggest hits in America and the public didn't seem to have time for any other comedy team.

The following year their success was acknowledged with a guest spot in a Hope and Crosby "Road" picture . . . *The Road To Bali*. Now Jerry reportedly started thinking of himself as another Chaplin and Dean started wondering how he came to be nothing more than a straightman.

In 1952, Wallis stuck to the formula. *Sailor Beware* was a blatant spin-off of *At War With The Army*. So much so that the original working title was *At Sea With The Navy*. The plot was no more complicated than this: Dean has rank. Jerry has problems. Some of the material in that film was written by John Grant, a man who spent many years writing for Abbott and Costello. And if the gags in *Sailor Beware* look exactly like some of the gags in Bud and Lou's *Buck Private*, it's no accident. Nor was the fact that their next film, *Jumping Jacks* should have been called *At War With The Parachute Brigade*. This one was so silly . . . complete with shadows on the sky backdrop when Dean and Jerry are hanging from their parachutes . . . that even the Army liked it. Twenty years later when *M*A*S*H* hit the screens, the Department of Defence cringed, and some posts actually outlawed the film from being shown in on-base theatres. But *Jumping Jacks* was right up the Army's street and Hal Wallis even sent a copy of a letter he received from an Army one-star General to the press. "I wish to express my appreciation ot Paramount Studios for the excellent motion picture *Jumping Jacks*," wrote Brig. Gen. Frank Dorn, then Deputy Chief of Information for the Department of the Army. "This motion picture is most entertaining. Of particular interest to us was the fact that the supporting actors portrayed their roles as theough they actually were members of the Parachute School." It's the best critique today the picture could possibly have.

Now firmly established as stars with six films, the partnership entered into a stormy "middle years" period. Between 1953 and 1953, they made six more films, but by this time the formula was becoming old hat and the tensions between Dean and Jerry were mounting and starting to take their toll. *The Stooge* seems silly today, and was probably just as silly in those days. Daniel Farson, reviewing the film for *Sight And Sound* made a special point of trying to sum up Dean's role. "His screen characterization is slick and cocksure, possessing all the unattractiveness of the professional charmer. He sings uninterestingly. He gave a convincing and unpleasant portrayal of a drunk in *The Stooge*, but otherwise his acting has been negligible." At the same time, the critics were happy with Jerry Lewis, although years later David Shipman writing about Jerry in *The Great Movie Stars* would have the insight to say, "Jerry Lewis falls down stairs and ladders, out of airplanes and windows and into holes and swimming pools. He is bullied by hotel clerks, waiters, cab drivers and passers-by. But he catapults back. There are millions of filmgoers who have never seen him. Like Rin Tin Tin and Elvis Presley, he appears in films devoted almost exclusively to himself."

That was certainly true in *Scared Stiff*, where Hal Wallis revised a Bob Hope-Paulette Goddard epic called *Ghost Breakers*. The best of it is Jerry's imitation of Carmen Miranda, and a return guest appearance by Hope and Crosby. *The Caddy* came about when one screen writer suggested to Jerry that they do a film where Jerry clowns as Dean is trying to play golf. Plot and storyline was not what this film was all about. Annoying Dean was what it turned out to be. Jerry would do his thing and that would be enough to steal any thunder Dean might have possessed. As Dean explained during the '60s in his interview with Italian journalist Oriana Fallaci, "I was doing nothing and I was eating my heart out. I sang a song and never got to finish the song. The camera would go over to him doing funny things, then it would come back to me when I'd finished. Everything was Jerry Lewis, Jerry Lewis, and I was a straight man. I was an idiot in every picture."

In all fairness, during *The Caddy*, Dean did get to do a number from beginning to end. It was *That's Amore*, and if the producers had listened to Dean, the song that became his first big-hit single would have been taken out of the film. Supposedly in those days Dean didn't like to learn new songs. When they gave him the words to *That's Amore*, he couldn't understand why they wouldn't simply let him sing one of his old standards. But this one was written for him and the film, and the producers insisted. He had little choice but to sing it. However, when they wanted him to record it as a single, he balked. They had to release the soundtrack version which, ironically enough in the face of Dean's opposition to the song, was his very first top of the charts record.

The next film, *Money From Home* was all about horse racing, and shot in 3-D, probably as a gimmick to make up for the weakness of the picture . . . although Sheldon Leonard playing the gangster is a great ham and his performance is very camp. Then came *Living It Up*, a revamp of an early classic titled *Nothing Sacred*. Looking back, they shouldn't have bothered.

Jerry Lewis in That's My Boy *(1951)*

(Right) Dean, Donna Reed and Jerry in The Caddy *(1953)*

The last of these "middle films" was *Three Ring Circus* and there are two things that make this one significant. Firstly, there is Elsa Lancaster as the bearded lady, and is she ever wonderful! Secondly, during the shooting, the newspapers rumored that this would be the team's last film. It seems the set was in constant turmoil with Dean and Jerry fighting.

At the same time, serious students of comedy were looking at the films of Martin and Lewis and drawing certain conclusions. One of the people who put them under a microscope was television personality Steve Allen in his book *The Funny Men*. Like most people, he figured Dean was just there to be a straightman for Jerry, "Of whom insanity is expected and hoped for. There is still much of a child in Jerry. On stage he does not revert to idiocy, he sometimes seems to be an idiot, and the effect is wonderfully, heart-warmingly hilarious." One of the special qualities that Allen saw in Lewis was Jerry's ability to recreate childish clowning. And Allen said that one of Jerry's major assets was, "His youthful, almost childish appearance. It allows him to indulge completely in the physical lunacies that have become his stock in trade. Milton Berle or Red Skelton may also take a pie in the face or fall into an orchestra pit, but somehow these older men have a

certain touch of stature and dignity under their clown's clothes." Lewis, on the other hand, managed his clowning without any dignity at all, making him the complete jester.

Of course, in later years, as Jerry aged, he seemed less and less childish, which might be one of the reasons his films as a single-star turned out the way they did. But in those days the fact that Jerry was heart-warmingly hilarious was about the last thing Dean Martin wanted to hear. The funnier everyone thought Jerry was, the more foolish Dean must have felt.

Trying to patch over that problem, Jerry told some wide-circulation magazines in the States, "People make a mistake when they think of me and me alone as the comedian of our team. If you reckon Dean is 'only a straightman' you're way off the beam. He sets up 60% of my gags. Without him I'm just a mimic." It probably sounded right at the time, except that setting up gags is exactly what a straight man is supposed to do.

The final four films happened quickly. *You're Never Too Young* was a remake of the Ray Milland-Ginger Rogers hit *The Major And The Minor*, with Dean doing the Milland part, and Jerry playing the Ginger Rogers role. *Artists And Models* was an all-right comedy . . . it still seems funny in parts . . . and gave Shirley

(Above) With Barbara Bates in The Caddy

(Right) Their last film, Hollywood Or Bust *(1956)*

MacLaine her cinema debut. The supporting cast included Eva Gabor, Anita Ekberg and Dorothy Malone. In *Pardners*, Dean and Jerry play cowboys. But Dean probably had to grit his teeth as he sang the title song which boasted of the way he and his pal would ride the trails together forever. The funniest bit in this picture is Jerry's pantomime of the gunslinger who twirls a six-shooter on his finger, tosses it into the air and lets it fall smartly into his holster. The difference between Jerry doing it and someone like John Wayne, is that Jerry did it without a gun . . . pretending . . . even dropping the invisible pistol several times. The script originally came from a Bing Crosby movie, *Rythmn On The Range*. The last picture was *Hollywood Or Bust*, about a pair of partners who were going to make it in the movies. On film they did. In real life it was the end.

Dean had enough. He felt he couldn't go on. The studio wanted them to make *The Delicate Delinquent*, with Dean playing a cop to support Jerry's role as star comic. Dean said no. Jerry said that if Dean wouldn't play the part, someone else would. Dean's often quoted answer was, "Start looking boy!"

At Paramount, they panicked. They felt they had too much money invested in Dean and Jerry, and too much to lose, if the team split up. The moguls called an emergency meeting of the inner cabinet. Somehow they had to talk Dean into making the film with Jerry. But Dean let them know in no uncertain terms exactly what he felt. They begged. And he replied, "Bullshit."

The break-up made front pages across the nation.

And for months everyone in America walked around saying, "Poor Dean.' Jerry, they knew, would easily turn into a superstar. But without Jerry, everyone wondered sympathetically, what would ever become of the singer from Steubenville?

The Films of Martin and Lewis

(All were produced by Hal Wallis for Paramount, although the credit in some acknowledges York Productions, a company formed by Martin and Lewis to produce films in association with Paramount. It was basically nothing more than a profit sharing scheme, as Wallis and Paramount had script approval over York's films for Martin and Lewis.)

My Friend Irma – 1949
My Friend Irma Goes West – 1950
At War With The Army – 1951
That's My Boy – 1951
Sailor Beware – 1952
Jumping Jacks – 1952
The Stooge – 1953
Scared Stiff – 1953
The Caddy – 1953
Money From Home – 1954

Living It Up – 1954
Three Ring Circus – 1954
You're Never Too Young – 1955
Artists and Models – 1955
Pardners – 1956
Hollywood or Bust – 1956

(In addition, Martin and Lewis as a team made one guest appearance in a Bob Hope and Bing Crosby picture, *The Road To Bali*, dated 1952)

Lemmon + Matthau

Lemmon & Matthau in The Fortune Cookie *(1966)*

The part-time teaming of Walter Matthau and Jack Lemmon is probably as off-beat a concept as the pairing itself was unlikely. Who knows why it works. Who knows what makes two guys so funny. Although in this case it's a good bet that the answer has a lot more to do with Matthau and Lemmon themselves than just good material.

They are obviously not a team in the strictest sense of the word . . . their names have never been in lights above the Roxy, six-shows-a-day, song and dance, a few gags thrown in between the bumps and grinds of Boom Boom Laverne. The two of them came from different worlds, totally different backgrounds. And they might well have stayed in their own separate worlds had Jack Lemmon not realised that Walter Matthau was a very special kind of comedian . . . and Walter Matthau not understood that by playing off the comic brilliance of Jack Lemmon, the sky was the limit.

Nor are they a team in the sense that they would or could never work alone. They can and mostly do. In fact, as a team, their output is miniscule. They've only done five films together, and in one of the five Lemmon never even shows his face in front of the camera. He directed. However, each of those five pictures is so special that Matthau and Lemmon can't be written off as merely a lucky yoking. Each of their films together is very much a classic team effort, filled with all the magic that happens when two actors turn onto each other as if they've been tossing lines back and forth for years.

Because of the nature of the movie business these days, teams are a rare breed. There's no place for them to learn how to be a team. Vaudeville and burlesque are bone-yards. Belushi and Aykroyd came from television, but that didn't last long enough to amount to what it might have and anyway, it's not everyone who can translate from a twenty-one inch screen into Cinemascope. The road from television to the movies is littered with corpses. So when it comes to learning how to be a team, the training grounds are gone. Redford and Newman may make a film or two together, but they're not really a team. They're Redford and Newman. Like all actors they're free agents who work together occasionally. Actors these days have to go it alone.

The exceptions are Matthau and Lemmon.

Both of them were stars in their own right before they even met. And both of them continue to command star-billing when they work alone. But it's when they work together that something very special happens. They work like a comedy team trained the way the Marx Brothers were, thinking like a team the way Laurel and Hardy did. Whether it's partially because they have put their egos to one side, or partially because, as close friends they simply enjoy working together . . . whatever happens, it comes down to this: the whole is more than the sum of the parts. What happens is something that neither one could do alone. What happens is cinema's most sophisticated comedy team.

Yet the odds of it happening realy were high against.

They literally had never met until their first film together.

Jack Lemmon was born in an elevator in Newton, Massachusetts in 1925. His handle at the time was John Uhler Lemmon III and, like many people who have numbers tacked onto the end of their names, he went to some of the *right* schools . . . the Phillips Academy and then Harvard. After graduation he served in the U.S. Navy for three years. Once that was out of the way he set his own course. He was going to be an actor. But according to a story he still loves to tell, his first task was getting some money from his father to go to New York to find acting jobs. His father was in the bakery business. "Dad would have loved me to enter his business, but all he said was 'You love acting? You need it? You must do it.' Then he said the greatest line I've ever heard in my life. He said, 'The day I can't find romance in a loaf of bread, I'll get out of the baking business.'"

With money and hope in his hands, he headed for New York, and his luck was good. The timing was right. The early '50s were good days for actors in the Big Apple. There might have been a dozen out of work actors on every street corner, but a lot of actors were working. Television was where the action was, and television was in New York.

Of course there were plays when he was a kid . . . drama at Harvard, a season of summer stock . . . but none of that mattered when he got to New York. He banged on doors and waited on tables and slowly started to get work. In five years he figures he might have appeared in as many as five hundred television shows. It made him very ready for Broadway, which came along in 1953 when he appeared in the entire eighteen performance run of *Room Service*. Just after that Columbia offered him a screen test and he made the trip west. His first film was *It Should Happen To You*, directed by George Cukor and starring Judy Holliday. Three films later he worked with Cagney and Fonda in *Mr. Roberts* and, as Ensign Pulver, he won himself the 1955 Oscar for Best Supporting Actor. But then he learned a new lesson about life as an actor. As he put it, "The problem I'd never anticipated is that, in film, success breeds unemployment. In other words, if you get a lead and it's good and it works, you can't just go and do a picture tomorrow. You have to find something on that same level". He learned it the hard way because it took him half a dozen films and four years before he found anything to match *Mr. Roberts*. This one was *Some Like It Hot*, and it was Lemmon's first effort with Billy Wilder.

A true Hollywood legend, Wilder is one of the masters of screen comedy. He also has to go down in the record books as Lemmon's first "partner". They hit it off in *Some Like It Hot* . . . that film is usually always included on somebody's all-time best list . . . and then a year later with *The Apartment*. In 1962 Blake Edwards stepped in to direct Lemmon in *The Days of Wine and Roses* and three years later in *The Great Race*, proving to the world that Lemmon was not only a splendid comic, but also a wonderful tragedian. In between there was Wilder again with *Irma La Douce*. By 1966 Jack Lemmon was very much a Hollywood heavyweight. And along came Wilder again. The story he wanted to do with Jack was called *The Fortune Cookie*.

Born in 1920, Walter Matthau was raised in poverty on New York's lower east side. His father walked out when Walter was just three years old and his mother supported the family by working as a seamstress. He pitched in by selling ice cream and sodas in Yiddish theatres. He also played bit parts when they came up. In those days he didn't take a serious interest in acting. After a time he left school and worked for a while as a basketball coach. Finally the war broke out and he enlisted. Discharged in 1945, he decided that maybe acting wasn't such a bad idea after all. So he enrolled in the Dramatic Workshop at New York's New School, and for the next several years, he didn't go very far. Yet in the early '50s he started to realize that he indeed had a certain kind of stage presence. Being 6 ft 3 in tall obviously helped. Yet that wasn't all of it. There was something about his face, and his eyes, and the way he moved and the way he spoke. As he himself has said, "I wasn't handsome. I didn't have good clothes. I used to wonder why people would hire me. Then it became apparent that when I got up on a stage, people wanted to look at me. What did I have to offer? I was a big, rugged-looking guy with a big, strong voice. There was that. Also I had a way of showing enormous ease and enormous power on stage, both of which were valuable in the theatre."

All of which combined to keep him working from his first Broadway success in 1955 . . . *Will Success Spoil Rock Hunter?* . . . to the one that really counted in 1965 . . . *The Odd Couple*.

During the intervening ten years, Matthau worked regularly on Broadway, did a bunch of television spots, and even a handful of films. In 1953 Billy Wilder had supposedly wanted to cast Matthau opposite Marilyn Monroe in *The Seven Year Itch* but Darryl Zanuck had never heard of Walter Matthau and that was the end of the discussion. As it was, Matthau made a good living playing the heavy in films like *The Kentuckian* with Burt Lancaster, and was so convincing as the villain that he almost found himself typed.

"I realized that directors in movies have mostly no idea of characterization," he said of Hollywood during those 1955-1965 visits. "They're cutters, technicians, people from families who are big in the business. You'd come in, no one would even introduce you to anyone, you'd start the most intimate kind of scene and you didn't know the person. So I started asking questions, holding the whole schedule up. I had to do that to get noticed, in order for them to say, 'There's that pain-in-the-ass actor who wants to know who he is, where he's coming from and why he's saying the lines. One of those artistic actors.'"

It must have worked because the moment Matthau scored a huge success in the Broadway version of Neil Simon's *The Odd Couple* . . . playing against the very talented Art Carney . . . Hollywood realized that he was not just some villain type but also a great comic.

116

And Wilder remembered him as well. He rang Matthau to say that a part was open for a film called *The Fortune Cookie*.

The planets had finally brought Lemmon and Matthau together.

The Fortune Cookie is the story of Harry Hinkle, a television cameraman who, while working a football game, has an unscheduled run-in with an over-zealous player. Hinkle is knocked unconscious and rushed to a hospital, where he eventually opens his eyes to find his lawyer brother-in-law standing nearby ready to sue the world. With promises of winning a fortune in court, Willie Gingrich convinces Hinkle to exaggerate the extent of his injuries to the point where Gingrich runs wild with greed of impending fortune and the football player responsible for the collision is near demented with guilt. Gingrich is merciless. But Hinkle has a last minute change of heart, abandons the scheme by making a "miracle recovery" and abruptly ends his brother's-in-law scheme.

Hinkle is a good role, but it's the straight man's role. Gingrich is the big part. And when Matthau realized that he was being tagged to play Gingrich, he couldn't believe it. The part was one that absolutely guaranteed stardom. There was no doubt about it, especially working opposite Lemmon. As the story is told, he was so shocked at landing the job that he supposedly went to Lemmon and said, "But I'm the one who will get all the laughs." Lemmon's answer was reported as, "It's about time."

It seems the two hit it off right away. They met on the set, discovered that they both shared a love of football and that broke the ice. Lemmon's unselfishness in letting Matthau "steal" the picture . . . "steal" might be a little strong, but it certainly comes close . . . together with his own talent as a hitherto unheralded straight man, made the film a winner. As Will Holtzman wrote in his biography of Lemmon, "*The Fortune Cookie* revealed that he was the best straight man in contemporary Hollywood. What is it Lemmon does? He doesn't. He doesn't upstage Matthau, he doesn't step on others' lines, he doesn't place his own humour above the film's. The classic Lemmon timing is in full flower, down to the last beat." Holtzman feels that the "chemistry" of the film was a mixture of Lemmon and Wilder. Looking at it these days it might be fairer to say that it was Lemmon and Matthau with Wilder as a chaser. In any case, Shyster Gingrich earned Walter Matthau his first Academy Award. He was named as the year's Best Supporting Actor. Although Shyster Gingrich also almost cost Walter Matthau his life. Halfway through the shooting of *The Fortune Cookie* Matthau suffered a heart attack. Production ground to a halt for seven weeks. No one knew if the picture would be scrapped or if someone could be put in to take over Matthau's role. In a performance worthy of an award, Matthau's wife, Carol managed to convince producers and studio execs. that her husband was on his way, any minute now, he'll be right here. She kept them at bay until he was ready to work again.

The picture did what everyone knew it would.

Matthau was now a movie star.

Within a year word went around Hollywood that Matthau and Lemmon would be teamed up a second time. And this time the film would be Matthau's home turf. Neil Simon wrote the screenplay of his own hit, Gene Saks directed, and *The Odd Couple* went before the cameras. Lemmon played Felix, the ever-so-neat recently divorced chum who moves in with Oscar . . . played both on stage and in the film by Matthau . . . the slob of a sportswriter who is more interested in what's happening at Yankee Stadium than washing last week's dishes. For Matthau, few roles could have been better

suited. Not only had he spent all those nights on Broadway living inside Oscar's skin, he had originally gotten the role because Neil Simon himself felt it was a natural one for Matthau. They met at a cocktail party in 1963 and when Simon spotted Matthau, he walked over to him and said, "You're gonna be in my next play." Matthau responded, "Who are you?" The rest, as they say, is history. During the Broadway run, Time Magazine gave Matthau straight-A marks. "Each of his character creations has a fine tuned completeness that leaves no room for Matthau the personality to peek through. A gimmick, a trademark, an image, Matthau

does not have. 'People either ask me, are you a television actor? or, are you from Erie, Pennsylvania?' " Time also quoted Simon with, "Matthau is the greatest instinctive actor I've ever seen." In addition to talent, Time decided, Matthau and Oscar were so close to being alike that the role of Oscar fitted Matthau like a glove. "Like Oscar in the play, Matthau is a natural born lounger, poker fan and sports buff. He is just the sort who would spray beer as he opened a can."

Matthau obviously agrees. He's called the part of Oscar, "One of those rare roles that come once in a lifetime, where the actor and character are a perfect fit."

And again, the unselfish Lemmon let Matthau have full run of the sound stage to do his thing. "I'd be remiss if I didn't mention my favourite leading lady," he told an interviewer years later. "Without a doubt it's Walter Matthau. He leads the pack by a country mile." To that he added, "Walter has talent that still hasn't been tapped. Films haven't yet touched on his depth." It's a theme he's repeated whenever anyone asks about his favourite actors. "It's touchy when you get to pick one over the other, because you can get either run over by a truck, or a producer, or hit by a leading lady. But I've never enjoyed working with any actor more than Walter Matthau in *The Odd Couple*. We have a great rapport. We're very close friends. And it's very exciting to work with him. If in the middle of a scene someone gets an idea, there's no hesitation, we just do it. *The Odd Couple* was a very lucky picture for me, of course, yet originally Paramount thought I would want to play Walter's part and Walter actually wanted to play my part. But the director said, 'No Walter, you're born for this part? . . . and he was."

The Odd Couple hit the movie houses around America and became an instant hit. It also reportedly filled Lemmon's bank accounts to the tune of $2 million, and while it might not have done that much for Matthau's . . . Lemmon got top billing and therefore top dollar . . . it certainly paid the rent. Time reviewed the film and called Matthau "America's finest comic actor," which seemed a fitting tribute, seeing as how they had only a few years before dubbed that same title on Lemmon.

Writing in the Los Angeles Times, critic Charles Champlin observed, "Lemmon gives a very straight and earnest performance as tormented Felix. In fact, he sets up Matthau for the pay-off lines in precisely the way he did in Billy Wilder's *The Fortune Cookie*. It's a kind of brinkmanship, but here I think it mostly works, laying a base of seriousness and reality on which the comedy builds and which lets it pay off. The usual critics term is 'finely judged' and I judge the Lemmon-Matthau relationship to have been finely judged for maximum laughs." Concluding his review Champlin said, "For what it's worth, I clocked 208 laughs, and I may have missed a couple. I don't know that it's a relevant movie, just damned funny."

And even today . . . with the play in repertory and the television spin-off in daytime reruns . . . the film is still very funny.

121

(Overleaf) Buddy, Buddy *(1981)*

The Front Page *(1974)*

Because the two weren't a team, because they both had their own identities, they followed their joint efforts with other solo films. Then came 1970, and an old friend approached Jack Lemmon with a project. The friend had bought the rights to a novel by Katherine Topkins, a story called *Kotch* about an old man's search for pride and his own identity. All the big studios had turned it down. But Lemmon loved it and immediately wanted to try his hand at directing. Using his name, he managed to swing a deal that, at least at first and on paper, looked terrific. Fredric March would play the lead. But then the moguls had second thoughts. Lemmon might be a fabulous actor but he had never directed before. He was therefore what is known in the business as a novice. On top of that, Fredric March was no longer a household name. His talent was indisputable but his box-office drawing power had gone. Ever the gentleman, March bowed out to help save the project and Lemmon turned to Matthau. Then only fifty years old, Walter agreed to play the part of a man who could have been his father. With Matthau signed, ABC came up with some money . . . low budget stuff . . . and everyone involved figured that was better than nothing. Lemmon's wife, Felicia Farr played Matthau's daughter-in-law . . . when the budget is low, hire your friends . . . and when the Oscar nominations were announced for the 1971 crop, *Kotch* was listed four times. Matthau was nominated for Best Actor, and although he didn't win the prize, his work in *Kotch*, directed by Lemmon, is a fine performance.

But this was not really the stuff of true comedy team work, and it took Billy Wilder to bring Matthau and Lemmon together on screen for two more outings. It was 1974 and Wilder with his screenwriting partner I. A. L. Diamond revised a Ben Hecht and Charles MacArthur play about the newspaper business. It had been filmed twice before . . . the first time in 1930, the second in 1940 . . . but in teaming Matthau and Lemmon, and adding Carol Burnett, *The Front Page* became a winner. Matthau was the editor, Walter Burns. Lemmon was his ace reporter, Hildy Johnson. The action is set in the '20s and the big story is the imminent execution of a convicted killer.

Burns is a double-dealing, sneaky, lying conman, and Hildy Johnson has had enough. He walks out. But just as he does, the killer escapes and lands in Johnson's lap. Burns manoeuvres Johnson into covering the story. When the commotion finally dies down, Johnson again tries to walk out, but Burns has no intention of letting his best reporter get away.

Deliberately kept short . . . the film comes in at just about 105 minutes . . . the comic pacing and punch never lets up. The speed of it all might even be called hectic. But the nose to nose confrontations of Matthau and Lemmon are so good that they seem proof positive that these two had, in some other life, tramped around the country as a pair of stand-up comics. As one reviewer put it, *"The Front Page* is an unblemished professional walk-through that does the material justice, and that is all the tribute that need be paid."

And again the two went off on their own, coming back together for the fifth time in Billy Wilder's *Buddy Buddy*.

Originally a play written for the French public, the script was turned into a wonderful film called *L'Emmerdeur*, which paired French star Lino Ventura with singer-turned-actor, Jacques Brel. The English title was *A Pain In The A*. Ventura plays a cold and calculating assassin who checks into a hotel in Montpellier where he plans to bump off a former gangland member about to testify before a Grand Jury. Brel is a clothes salesman in the next room trying to commit suicide. Unfortunately, Brel is a hopeless type who can't even get that right, and out of sympathy Ventura saves him. Then Ventura can't get rid of him and in the end that costs him his hit. Wilder and Diamond liked the idea so much that they updated and Americanised it. Lemmon is the man trying to commit suicide and Matthau is the sympathetic assassin.

"I never say no to Billy Wilder," Matthau explained about accepting the heavy's role, even if that heavy is a kind one. "As a matter of fact, I would have signed up to star for Billy with Jack Lemmon without reading the script. Wilder is my favourite director."

The feelings must be mutual because at the same time Wilder said, "Matthau is a palette with every colour you want. He has enough talent to make four big stars. He's as deft at comedy as he is at drama. And there's only one Matthau. Some stars can be interchanged. But when a part is specifically written for Matthau, such as his role in *Buddy Buddy*, then I believe that no one else can fill that role. He's very uniquely distinctive. He has a walk all his own and a face all his own. "He is a good actor, very economical. He knows how to get the maximum out of close-ups. For all the trouble and aggravation he puts me through, I wish I could have him for my next fifty pictures.

As far as Lemmon was concerned, "I can say of Walter and Billy what a character in *Tribute* says of Scottie Templeton. They can take a hamburger and make you feel like you were at a banquet." But then *Buddy Buddy* wasn't the easiest of banquets for Lemmon. In fact, it might have been one of his most gruelling films because of all the stunts he had to do. "I'm a lover, not an athlete," he is known to have groaned on the set. "First, I attempted suicide by hanging myself from a pipe in the bathroom. The pipe broke, I fell into the tub and for the next two weeks I played all of my scenes sopping wet. Next I had to climb out on a narrow ledge of a three-story facade on location in Riverside, California. Of course there was a belt with a hidden wire to protect me, but I do think that being over fifty I'm a bit too old to be doing the Peter Pan bit for the first time."

Then came the scene where he had to burn some ropes off his hands after being tied to a chair. Bound and gagged, he had to hop in the chair across the room to a wall heater. Naturally the heater had to be on. Crew stood by to pull him away if he got into trouble, but no one could tell if his moans were real or not. It was a dangerous stunt, and everyone realized it. Luckily no

damage was done. At one point he also had to fall over backward while tied to the chair. "Young bones can take this kind of torture, but I was sore for days." Then there was the scene where Lemmon had to go down a laundry chute, head first. "Even as a kid, slides were never my thing. Matthau pushes me down the chute first and I'm supposed to scream on the way down. Believe me, it didn't require much acting."

It's one thing for him to say it . . . "It didn't require much acting" . . . it's another thing for anyone to believe him. The true actor-as-artist is one who makes it all look easy. And Lemmon is certainly one of the very few with that kind of talent. As a serious actor, his range is enormous. From *The Days Of Wine And Roses* to winning the Cannes Film Festival Best Actor award for his work in *Missing*, few actors have had as long and as illustrious a career. Yet after making *Buddy Buddy* he told one reporter, "People do remember me for the humour rather than the tears. That's okay, I like to make people laugh. My own heroes were Laurel and

fascinates me, is that you lack the one precious vital ingredient an actor needs. An audience. You must time the laughs in your mind so that you don't go on talking while the people in the cinema are still laughing. You can't stare out of the screen and wait.''

And in that remark might come one of the clues to the reason that Matthau and Lemmon click. Maybe there's something that happens when one member of a team hits a line . . . a kind of glint in the eyes from the other half of the team . . . to say, it's all right, that was funny, do the next one now.

Matthau himself is fairly flippant about film acting . . . most serious stage trained performers are. He calls it, ''Retirement acting. You just give an exhibition of your former skills. Films are piecework. You do a little job. Then you do it over and over again. You don't even have to learn your lines. You do so many rehearsals, you learn them on the set.''

When it comes to discussing his own image and his skills as an actor however, he's just as pointed. ''The one thing I'm most serious about is my comedy.'' He feels it is not the opposite of drama but rather a subhead of drama. ''Tragedy is the other main subheading.'' But then he is the kind of an actor who works for what he knows is the best performance possible, and doesn't care what anyone else thinks. ''Why should I care? Hollywood is a town full of idiots. Half the people who view movies are idiots, and the men and women who review them are idiots.'' When it comes to his own image, he's been known to say, ''Anybody with a big nose, little lips and beady eyes looks like me. It's been said I remind people of their favourite uncle.'' Yet Lemmon is the man who has often said that Matthau has ''The greatest single face in the world as an actor. It is the map of every human emotion.''

And Lemmon should know. He's laughed at that mug, shouted at it, stared at it, loved it and hated it through five films. He's made it react and reacted to it. He's stared into those beady eyes and waited for the glint that's told him, now the next one. He might even in some ways think of that face as the face of his brother. Although Matthau himself told Photoplay Magazine, ''I wouldn't say we're like brothers, but we're very chummy cousins. We're too different to be brothers, but we have the best chemistry this side of Tracy and Hepburn.''

And nothing more need be added to that.

(Overleaf) 'Babe' Hardy bows out.

Hardy, Keaton, Chaplin, W. C. Fields, but I never knowingly modelled myself on any of them. I never had a basic desire to be a comic actor, you know. It's just that when I first went into movies my early films were comedies and they seemed to work.'' He went on to explain, ''The one true fact about comedy is that you have to play it deadly serious, even something as crazy and farcical as this.'' And to that he added an actor's insight into the world of playing comedy. ''One of the toughest things about screen comedy, something that

The Films Of Matthau and Lemmon
The Fortune Cookie – 1966 – United Artists. (English title was *Meet Whiplash Willie*)
The Odd Couple – 1968 – Paramount
Kotch (Lemmon as director) – 1971 – Cinerama
The Front Page – 1974 – Universal
Buddy Buddy – 1981 – MGM